OVERCOME
BY THE WORD

by
Roger L. Bilbrey

© Copyright 2019 –Roger L. Bilbrey
Tree of Life Coaching
ISBN: 978-1-7332018-6-5

All rights reserved. This book is protected by the copyright laws of the United States of America. This book, nor any portion, may not be copied or reprinted. Permission may be granted upon written request.

Printed in the United States of America
Roger Bilbrey & Associates---Publisher

ALL SCRIPTURES ARE FROM THE KJV OF THE BIBLE

Table of Contents

Ch. 1 Why is the Word Important................... 3

Ch. 2 Overcoming Words for January............... 8

Ch. 3 Overcoming Words for February............22

Ch. 4 Overcoming Words for March...............37

Ch. 5 Overcoming Words for April.................54

Ch. 6 Overcoming Words for May..................71

Ch. 7 Overcoming Words for June.................87

Ch. 8 Overcoming Words for July................101

Ch. 9 Overcoming Words for August............116

Ch. 10 Overcoming Words for September.......131

Ch. 11 Overcoming Words for October..........145

Ch. 12 Overcoming Words for November.......160

Ch. 13 Overcoming Words for December.......175

Conclusion...189

Why is God's Word Important?

Chapter 1

Words are probably one of the most important things in life besides food, water, and shelter. It is how we communicate with others, our desires, dreams, hopes, directions, and so much more.

They are so important that we have developed ways for people who can't see or hear to understand and communicate their needs as well through sign language and Braille.

One of the biggest struggles that I see in the life of believers is their walk with God. We live in a world that is increasingly turning away from the standards of the Christian belief, that this nation was founded upon. So, how can a Christian live life under all the pressure from peers, society, and the workplace?

Well, the hard fact is, no matter what you do, there will always be a struggle between good and evil. Satan and his demons will always be there trying to make you slip up, or worse, turn away from God.

But I have good news!!! God loves us so much that He gave us 66 Books, approx. 31,173 verses and 783,137 rough word count in the King James Bible, to help us better live our lives with more victory and purpose.

One of the reasons the Bible has given these is so we can be stronger to fight the enemy. Let me give you a couple of them now.

First, the Bible says in Psalm 119:11 "Thy word have I hid in mine heart, that I might not sin against thee." This verse seems to imply, that if we will not only read the Word of God but try to memorize it and internalize it, that it will help us overcome the enemy.

Christ gave us the perfect example of this when He was tempted by Satan. If you remember, every time that Satan would try and get Christ to sin, Christ would fight back with scriptures from the Word.

I believe Christ allowed this story to be told in the Bible, to show His followers how to handle situations when Satan is coming to try and make us fall.

Another powerful verse is found in Psalm 119:105, which says, "Thy word is a lamp unto my feet, and a light unto my path."

With this verse, it implies when we need guidance in our lives, we can always find the answer in God's Word. But the only way to do that is to read it!

It doesn't matter how old you are. It doesn't matter how much money you have. It doesn't matter how powerful in a position you are. It doesn't matter what you are going through; you need the Word of God to help you walk through life and make the right decisions. Without it, you might find yourself

going down the wrong path that will lead t
destruction.

For this reason, and especially for today's
adults, I have compiled some of my favorite
you with your daily walk with God.

For every month of the year and every day of that month, there is a scripture with a small comment. The comments are not designed to be some deep theological debate, but just something for you to think about.

I purposely didn't put the name of the day of the weeks, so that this book can be used year after year. There is no way you can remember all the verses in it, so I recommend you do just that; read it yearly.

If you really want to be a better Christian, I believe if you follow this schedule, you will find your life being closer to God and His perfect Will in your life. Here is my suggestion on how to accomplish this.

First, I believe you should read five chapters in Psalms and 1 chapter in Proverbs each day. This will allow you to read both books 12 times a year. To me, there are no other books in the Bible that give better instructions on how to walk in this life.

After you have read the five verses in Psalms and 1 verse in Proverbs, I believe you should then read the verse of the day and the notes that are with it.

Once you have done that, you should take a few minutes to be in a quiet place, and spend some time thinking about what you just read and how it can be applied to your life. You only need 5 minutes or so to do this.

I hope this book will be not only a blessing to you but the beginning of a new and closer walk with God.

I also wanted to mention why I had this desire to write this book. I have been a part of the Harvest Baptist Church in Jonesboro GA, with Pastor Dr. Joe Arthur for a few years now. I have been impressed with how spiritual, and on fire, the youth and young adults in that church are.

Sunday after Sunday, you see them really getting into the preaching of God's Word. You see them rushing to the altar for themselves and others, even during the song portion of the service. You see them active in going out to do personal ministry as well.

Then I moved to Florida for a year. I started going to Seagate Baptist Church in Naples with Pastor Glenn Wiggins, and to my surprise, I saw the same thing with his youth and young adults.

This doesn't just happen. This is a result of good sound preaching. It comes from sound doctrine as well. It comes from not compromising the church's values to draw a crowd, but rather trust in God. It shows that if you follow the leadership of God's direction, you will have strong Christians and you don't need all the lights, loud music and special programs to do it.

All of that being said, I chose to write this book as a thank you for those young adults and wanted to give them a little something of my appreciation. I would also say that if you are ever around the area of those two churches, you should stop by and enjoy the presence and power of God.

If you have some young people that you are proud of, or maybe some that are beginning to walk away from God and need to get closer to Him, I encourage you to get them a copy of this book.

We need to invest in our youth. They are America's future and the future of spreading the Gospel of Christ. They get enough of being talked bad about. Let's share with them the joy of serving the Lord and brag on them for their efforts in trying to be a better person.

I believe it will not only help them but older adults as well if they will take the time to read and meditate on the verses that are inside the pages of this book.

If while reading this book, you have questions or feel the need to understand God and Salvation better, feel free to write to us via our website at www.treeoflifecoaching.org. Someone will respond quickly to help you further your understanding of God's Word.

So, are you ready to Overcome by the Word? Then let's get started!

Overcoming Words for January
Chapter 2

Day 1. 1 Timothy 4:12
"Let no man despise thy youth; but be thou an example of the believers, in word, in conversation, in charity, in spirit, in faith, in purity."

Thought of the day: It doesn't matter how old you are, you can still be mighty in both an example in your life to others and in your walk with God. There are many examples like David, who as just a young lad, defeated a giant that even the King was afraid of. Don't let your age stop you from doing all you can do in life and for God. Be an example for all ages to look up to.

Day 2. Jeremiah 1:17
"Thou, therefore, gird up thy loins, and arise, and speak unto them all that I command thee: be not dismayed at their faces, lest I confound thee before them."

Thought of the day: Never be fearful to speak God's Word. Be brave and proud that He chose you to speak for Him. It is a privilege and an honor to do that! In our world today; we need people who will speak the truth. Be prepared to do what God wants you to do.

Day 3. Romans 12:2
"And be not conformed to this world: but be ye transformed by the renewing of your mind, that ye may prove what is that good, and acceptable, and perfect, will of God."

Thought of the day: Decisions and actions that will affect your life, come from your mind. Therefore, make sure you have the right thinking. Not stinking thinking. When we allow images and thoughts of this world in our minds, it takes root and tries to grow. The power to transform only comes from God and being obedient to Him, but it is also from guarding what our eyes and ears allow into our minds. When the wrong thought comes in your mind, immediately resist it and focus on something that God has said that can give you the strength to overcome whatever it is that Satan is trying to defile you with.

Day 4. Philippians 4:13
"I can do all things through Christ, which strengtheneth me."

Thought of the day: This verse is often misinterpreted. It is not so much that we can DO all things, but that we can BEAR all things. Another word, if God brought you to it, God will and can bring you through it.

Day 5. James 4:7
"Submit yourselves therefore to God. Resist the devil, and he will flee from you."

Thought of the day: When you try to obey God in ALL things, He will give you a supernatural power to overcome the enemy. If you are in God's Will, you will have power over the enemy. He was defeated at the Cross, and by the Blood of Jesus Christ, we can defeat him too. Don't let him make you fearful, use God's Word to defeat him. At times you are weak, also lean on other believers to help you through those times.

Day 6. Ecclesiastes 11:9
"Rejoice, O young man, in thy youth; and let thy heart cheer thee in the days of thy youth, and walk in the ways of thine heart, and in the sight of thine eyes: but know thou, that for all these things God will bring thee into judgment."

Thought of the day: It is not true that you can't have fun being a Christian, the key is to walk in God's ways and not fleshly pleasures. Then you will have great joy and happiness, both in your youth and your older years with no regrets or wasted years. There is a great, TRUE joy when serving Christ fully and abstaining from evil.

Day 7. John 14:14
"If ye shall ask anything in my name, I will do it."

Thought of the day: This verse is often misused. If you are walking with God and obeying Him, you will only want what He desires. Then you can ask Him for things in His Will, and He will give them to you according to His Will. If He doesn't give you what you want, it is for your good.

Day 8. 1 Corinthians 6:9-11
"Know ye not that the unrighteous shall not inherit the kingdom of God? Be not deceived: neither fornicators, nor idolaters, nor adulterers, nor effeminate, nor abusers of themselves with mankind, Nor thieves, nor covetous, nor drunkards, nor revilers, nor extortioners, shall inherit the kingdom of God. And such were some of you: but ye are washed, but ye are sanctified, but ye are justified in the name of the Lord Jesus, and by the Spirit of our God."

Thought of the day: When you have become a Christian, you need to stand out from the rest of the world. All that the world offers will bring pain eventually. You have the power through Christ Jesus to overcome these things and avoid that pain and agony that comes with the world's bidding. I promise you; you are not missing out of anything! If you are truly born again, sin will no longer have the power over you, but you can overcome the temptation through Christ. If you fail, He will forgive you and cleanse you upon asking. Before you became a believer, you may have been a slave to some of those things. Even after you became a believer, you may have done some of them. The difference is, you no longer enjoy them without conviction, and they can't hold you year after year doing them.

Day. 9 Ecclesiastes 12:1
"Remember now thy Creator in the days of thy youth, while the evil days come not, nor the years draw nigh when thou shalt say, I have no pleasure in them;"

Thought of the day: Begin serving God at an early age and don't depart from it, because once you do, you will find yourself regretting it when you get older. As the old saying goes, sin will take you farther than you want to go, stay longer than you want to stay and pay more than you want to pay.

Day 10. Acts 5:29
"Then Peter and the other apostles answered and said, we ought to obey God rather than men."

Thought of the day: No matter who or by what authority a person has; if they tell you to do something against God's Word… Obey God instead!!! He is the ultimate authority!

Day 11. James 1:13
"Let no man say when he is tempted, I am tempted of God: for God cannot be tempted with evil, neither tempteth He any man:"

Thought of the day: No matter what the world says about God making you a certain way, as to how you do or feel about something that is against God, don't believe it. It is the enemy that causes us to go against God's principles, and it was the Sin in the garden that caused the division of good and evil. Stop blaming God, and know where the source is coming from. God also can, and will, give you the power to overcome those temptations by putting your faith, trust, and obedience to Him.

Day 12. Isaiah 60:1
"Arise, shine; for thy light is come, and the glory of the Lord is risen upon thee."

Thought of the day: If you are a believer in Christ, every morning should be the start of a bright day, knowing that He is in full control! Share the light that you have within to all you come in contact with today!

Day. 13. 1 Peter 3:3-4
"Whose adorning let it not be that outward adorning of plaiting the hair, and of wearing of gold, or of putting on of apparel; But let it be the hidden man of the heart, in that which is not corruptible, even the ornament of a meek and quiet spirit, which is in the sight of God of great price."

Thought of the day: Have you ever met someone who had outward beauty, by once you got to know them, they lost that beauty? On the other hand, have you ever met someone who wasn't all that attractive, but once you got to know them, they appeared beautiful? My mom always said, "pretty is as pretty does." Beauty doesn't come from the outside, and if the outside is beautiful, one day, it will fade. But if a person has beauty on the inside, it will make them beautiful on the outside as well!

Day 14. John 8:36
"If the Son, therefore, shall make you free, ye shall be free indeed."

Thought of the day: If you feel bound and can't find the way out, you will only find it in Christ. He alone has the power and authority to set the captives free!!! Also, it is important to make sure that we are not living in sin, as sin alone will put you in bondage.

Day 15. 2 Chronicles 20:21-22
"And when he had consulted with the people, he appointed singers unto the Lord, and that should praise the beauty of holiness, as they went out before the army, and to say, Praise the Lord; for his mercy endureth forever. And when they began to sing and to praise, the Lord set ambushments against the children of Ammon, Moab, and mount Seir, which were come against Judah; and they were smitten."

Thought of the day: No matter how tough and impossible the battle, go ahead and give God praise because through your praise, His power will be released to defeat your enemy. Praise during the trial is an act of faith, trusting that God is going to deliver you, even though you can't see it now. That's the Faith God desires us to have.

Day 16. Luke 22:31-32
"And the Lord said, Simon, Simon, behold, Satan hath desired to have you, that he may sift you as wheat: But I have prayed for thee, that thy faith fail not: and when thou art converted, strengthen thy brethren."

Thought of the day: Satan hates every one of God's children. He wants to kill, steal, and destroy. But, isn't it good to know, that Christ loves us so much that He is keeping a watchful eye over us and making intercession on our behalf? Not only that, but He will also give us the power to overcome. But, if we fail, He will forgive us when we ask and repent. We should then teach and warn others about the traps of the Devil that we have fallen in, so they can try to avoid the same pitfalls.

Day 17. John 3:17
"For God sent not his Son into the world to condemn the world; but that the world through him might be saved."

Thought of the day: Unlike what the world tries to say about God, that He is unjust and mean; God has from the beginning of time, tried to make it easy for us to live for Him. He doesn't want to judge anyone or send them to Hell. That is man's choice and man's alone. Christ came not to judge us but make a way for us to be free from the sin debt that we owed to God, by shedding His Blood on Calvary. If you believe and accept that Blood for your Sins, you will be in good relationship with God and will spend eternity with Him.

Day 18. Jeremiah 29:11
"For I know the thoughts that I think toward you, saith the Lord, thoughts of peace, and not of evil, to give you an expected end."

Thought of the day: God has good plans in store for you. They may not seem that way at the moment, but in time, you will see it was best. Isn't it awesome to know that a God that created everything, cares enough to have a plan for your life?

Day 19. Joshua 1:9
"Have not I commanded thee? Be strong and of a good courage; be not afraid, neither be thou dismayed: for the Lord thy God is with thee whithersoever thou goest."

Thought of the day: When it seems, you are fighting a battle alone, it's good to know that God is right by your side always to help you along. We should never fear what comes our way, as Christ has already won the battle for us!

Day 20. Numbers 13:32
"And they brought up an evil report of the land which they had searched unto the children of Israel, saying, The land, through which we have gone to search it, is a land that eateth up the inhabitants thereof; and all the people that we saw in it are men of a great stature."

Thought of the day: God told the people of Israel, to go and conquer a land that could take care of their needs. Instead of just doing what God says, they decided to go and search the land to see how hard it would be to take it. When they saw all the people and how big they were, their hearts were fearful. So, they came and told the people of Israel what they saw and gave the report that they probably wouldn't be able to conquer them. God many times might send you somewhere to fight a battle that in the flesh seems impossible. But what they failed to understand and us too, if we fear; It is not us that is going to fight the battle, the battle is the Lords, and He will defeat the enemy. We just need to obey and do what He says. Whose report are you going to believe? The report of the enemy, or the voice of God?

Day 21. Micah 6:8
"He hath shewed thee, O man, what is good; and what doth the Lord require of thee, but to do justly, and to love mercy, and to walk humbly with thy God?"

Thought of the day: God has shown the path to walk. If we want to have peace and contentment, then we need to walk in that direction. "This is the way, walk ye in it" Isa. 30:31.

Day 22. Deuteronomy 6:6-7
"And these words, which I command thee this day, shall be in thine heart: And thou shalt teach them diligently unto thy children, and shalt talk of them when thou sittest in thine house, and when thou walkest by the way, and when thou liest down, and when thou risest up."

Thought of the day: It is our job as parents, or as family members, to teach the others how to live for God and what His Word says. We should not only teach them by our words, but also, by the way, we live it. Action speaks so much louder than words. We should show ourselves as Christians 24/7 365 days of the year!

Day 23. Amos 8:11-13
"Behold, the days come, saith the Lord God, that I will send a famine in the land, not a famine of bread, nor a thirst for water, but of hearing the words of the Lord: And they shall wander from sea to sea, and from the north even to the east, they shall run to and fro to seek the word of the Lord, and shall not find it. In that day shall the fair virgins and young men faint for thirst."

Thought of the day: The Bible warns that treacherous times are coming, and many will faint because of the lack of truth. But thank God we don't have to be in that number thirsting for truth or desiring the bread of life because we serve the one who is the Living Water and who is the Bread of Life! "Come taste and see that the Lord is GOOD!

Day 24. 2 Timothy 3:16-17
"All scripture is given by inspiration of God, and is profitable for doctrine, for reproof, for correction, for instruction in righteousness: That the man of God may be perfect, thoroughly furnished unto all good works."

Thought of the day: God has given us His Word so that we ourselves can live a good life, and also be able to gently and lovingly lead others who may be in sin to a better life in Christ. Are you not just reading the Word, but being the Word in front of others? Also, be careful not to judge others, that is God and God's only, job.

Day 25. Isaiah 1:18
"Come now, and let us reason together, saith the Lord: though your sins be as scarlet, they shall be as white as snow; though they be red like crimson, they shall be as wool."

Thought of the day: Isn't it wonderful, that no matter how dirty you have gotten by wallowing in the world's filth. God can and will wash and cleanse you afresh if you will just turn to Him. 1 John 3:1a "Behold, what manner of love the Father hath bestowed upon us."

Day 26. Isaiah 1:19-20
"If ye be willing and obedient, ye shall eat the good of the land: But if ye refuse and rebel, ye shall be devoured with the sword: for the mouth of the Lord hath spoken it."

Thought of the day: Not only will God clean us up when we get dirty as we learned yesterday, but He gives us a choice to decide if we want His blessings or not. If we want His blessings, we must follow His teachings.

Day 27. Luke 10:10-11
"But into whatsoever city ye enter, and they receive you not, go your ways out into the streets of the same, and say, Even the very dust of your city, which cleaveth on us, we do wipe off against you: notwithstanding be ye sure of this, that the kingdom of God is come nigh unto you".

Thought of the day: We, as believers, when sharing God's Word, don't have to be pushy and obnoxious in doing so. We need to warn them in love, of the wrath to come. But understand, don't lose heart when they reject it. They rejected Christ also. We are not responsible for the results, just the sharing of the Gospel.

Day 28. Mark 16:16
"He that believeth and is baptized shall be saved; but he that believeth not shall be damned."

Thought of the day: The most important thing that you will ever do in your life is to know that you know that you know that you have eternal life. It is not joining the church. It's not because your mom and dad are saved. It's not in being baptized. It is not because of your good works, but it is trusting and believing in Christ and His blood that paid for your sin debt. Have you done that? If not, do it today! Remember, you can be saved and not baptized. Being baptized is just an outward sign of an inward change.

Day 29. Matthew 19:20
"The young man saith unto him, all these things have I kept from my youth up: what lack I yet?"

Thought of the day: This verse is talking about a young man that wanted to purchase salvation, and Christ gave him a list of things to do, which the young man said he had kept. Most likely he hadn't, but Jesus was trying to make a point that with all his good works, he still was lacking if he wasn't willing to do one particular thing; To forsake all and follow

Christ. The only way to make it to Heaven is not trusting in what you do or have, but surrounding it all to Christ and giving Him your all and all. You can't buy your way to Heaven; the price has already been paid and that, through Christ Jesus Blood.

Day 30. Matthew 5:14-16
"Ye are the light of the world. A city that is set on an hill cannot be hid. Neither do men light a candle, and put it under a bushel, but on a candlestick; and it giveth light unto all that are in the house. Let your light so shine before men, that they may see your good works, and glorify your Father which is in heaven."

Thought of the day: The old saying is true; You might be the only Bible some people read. Do you live your life in a way that others will know that you have Christ inside of you without you saying a word? If not, why not? Let your light shine in this dark world so others can see the way!

Day 31. Isaiah 48:17
"Thus saith the Lord, thy Redeemer, the Holy One of Israel; I am the Lord thy God which teacheth thee to profit, which leadeth thee by the way that thou shouldest go."

Thought of the day: Economics can teach us how to make money and prosper, but only God can teach us not only how to make money and prosper, but how to prosper in all aspects of our life. Learn from Him.

Overcoming Words for February

Chapter 3

Day 1. 1 Corinthians 10:13
"There hath no temptation taken you but such as is common to man: but God is faithful, who will not suffer you to be tempted above that ye are able; but will with the temptation also make a way to escape, that ye may be able to bear it."

Thought of the day: Christ loved us so much, that He was tempted like every person, yet without sin. Because of that, He not only made it possible that we could escape the temptation, but He also has compassion for us because He knows the struggle. You are no different from any other person. We all struggle with sin. Don't let the enemy tell you otherwise. When the temptation comes, look around, you will find a way of escape, but it is up to you to take it.

Day 2. Romans 13:11
"And that, knowing the time, that now it is high time to awake out of sleep: for now is our salvation nearer than when we believed."

Thought of the day: No one can deny that we are living in the last days. It is more important now than ever before, regardless of your age, to stop playing the Christian life and live it. Christ coming is near, and we have no time to waste to do His Will. It's time to get fully in the game. Let's use the armor that God has given and fight the good fight until the end.

Day 3. Romans 8:1-2
"There is therefore now no condemnation to them which are in Christ Jesus, who walk not after the flesh, but after the Spirit. For the law of the Spirit of life in Christ Jesus hath made me free from the law of sin and death."

Thought of the day: It is not by our works, but Christ work on Calvary that we are free from our sins. That doesn't, however, relieve us of the responsibility to do what is right in His sight. Don't take what Christ did lightly. He paid a high price for your redemption and adoption. You should show how much you appreciate that by the life you live for Him.

Day 4. Isaiah 55:6
"Seek ye the Lord while he may be found, call ye upon him while he is near:"

Thought of the day: In order to seek the Lord, we must abandon our evil ways and repent. He will not be found while we live in sin. When we are in sin, we have moved away from Him, not that He has moved away from us. But, if we are away from Him, all we need to do is repent of our sins and call on Him. He will be right there waiting to rescue us. Don't wait too late to call on Him; however, once the death angel comes, it will be too late to repent.

Day 5. 1 Peter 5:7
"Casting all your care upon him; for he careth for you."

Thought of the day: Do you have a burden you seem not able to bear? Do you often feel like no one in the world cares what you are going through? Christ wants to make that burden easier and let you know that He cares. Pray a prayer to Him today and ask for that help. The King of Kings and Lord of Lords really cares for you!

Day 6. Acts 26:14
"And when we were all fallen to the earth, I heard a voice speaking unto me, and saying in the Hebrew tongue, Saul, why persecutest thou me? It is hard for thee to kick against the pricks."

When you read of accounts of supernatural events in the Bible, often the people who viewed it, fell to the ground in fear. This example seems to be just a voice, with a bright light. When God spoke on the mountain, the earth shook. God sometimes uses these supernatural events to stir our hearts or get our attention. Here, He used it to get Paul to understand, that even though he thought he was doing God's will; He was actually fighting against God. If you fight against God, you are in a losing battle. You might as well surrender, and that will help alleviate at least the problems you will face by disobedience.

Day 7. James 4:8
"Draw nigh to God, and he will draw nigh to you. Cleanse your hands, ye sinners; and purify your hearts, ye double minded."

Thought of the day: A lot is being said in this short verse. When you feel that God is not answering or far away, it is not Him who has left; it's you. He promised that if we come to Him, He will meet us. God is a gentleman and will not force Himself on anyone. Then He instructs us to try and live clean and keep our hearts pure. This can only be done through daily Bible reading, prayer and the power of the Holy Spirit. He is also calling the sinner to repentance. Now is the accepted time! Do it today!

Day 8. John 16:33
"These things I have spoken unto you, that in me ye might have peace. In the world ye shall have tribulation: but be of good cheer; I have overcome the world."

Thought of the day: Many people, when they see all the troubles that surround them, get fearful. They see the worst and imagine the worst. The believer should never focus on what is around them, but rather on the one who can change any situation and who has our back. God is always in control, even when the world or our life is out of control. Keep your eyes on Him, as Peter did when he walked upon the water. If you keep your eyes on Him, you won't sink.

Day 9. John 3:16
"For God so loved the world, that he gave his only begotten Son, that whosoever believeth in him should not perish, but have everlasting life."

Thought of the day: This simple verse that most of us learned while children, holds true today. To me, it is one of the best verses in the Bible to remember. We should never forget just how much Christ loved us. This should make us more determined to serve Him more than ever. It is through Him, and only Him, we can have salvation.

Day 10. Isaiah 41:10
"Fear thou not; for I am with thee: be not dismayed; for I am thy God: I will strengthen thee; yea, I will help thee; yea, I will uphold thee with the right hand of my righteousness."

Thought of the day: It is hard not to be fearful at times. But, if we can remember, God is the one that created everything and keeps it all going. Surely God can handle what problems we have when we see what all He controls now.

Day 11. 1 John 3:18
"My little children, let us not love in word, neither in tongue; but in deed and in truth."

Thought of the day: Sometimes, when people say they love you, it is shallow with little substance. The word love is used so loosely today. But love is an action word. It is shown, more than spoken. It is not what we say; it's what we do that shows our love.

Day 12. James 1:5
"If any of you lack wisdom, let him ask of God, that giveth to all men liberally, and upbraideth not; and it shall be given him."

Thought of the day: There is a difference between knowledge and wisdom. You can obtain knowledge by going to school, but the only way to get wisdom is to understand how to use the knowledge you have in the right way. When you can't understand what to do in a certain situation, turn to the one who has all understanding, and He has promised He would give you the wisdom you need. That is more valuable than any school or amount of money can be.

Day 13. Colossians 3:23
"And whatsoever ye do do it heartily, as to the Lord, and not unto men;"

Thought of the day: You might not feel you have the best job or amount to much in life. But no matter where you are, be the best you can be at it. We give and show God honor when we strive to be the best in all we do. It's not what you do, but how you do it that counts. Even if your job may only be cleaning toilets, be the best toilet cleaner there is. God will reward it.

Day 14. Philippians 4:6-7
Be careful for nothing; but in every thing by prayer and supplication with thanksgiving let your requests be made known unto God. And the peace of God, which passeth all understanding, shall keep your hearts and minds through Christ Jesus."

Thought of the day: Many times, we rush into something or buy something without giving it any thought whatsoever. Then we find that we made a mistake and should have waited, or not done it at all. We should pray about everything we have to make a decision on, to make sure it is in God's Will. Go ahead and give Him thanks for the answer no matter what that answer may be. You will find in time that God made the right decision for you.

Day 15. Ephesians 2:10
"For we are his workmanship, created in Christ Jesus unto good works, which God hath before ordained that we should walk in them."

Thought of the day: It is only human nature for us to want to do our own thing. But we must remember, we are not our own, we have been bought with a price and we have a purpose of fulfilling God's destiny in our lives. If you have trusted Christ, then you have decided on your own, to be His bondservant. That means you have on your own accord, decided to always do what He wants you to do and serve Him till the day you die. He is a good taskmaster and will reward you greatly.

Day 16. 1 Corinthians 6:18
"Flee fornication. Every sin that a man doeth is without the body; but he that committeth fornication sinneth against his own body."

Thought of the day: God made mankind to desire a relationship with the opposite sex, but only in the guidelines of marriage. When we don't obey God in this, it opens the door to all kinds of sexually transmitted diseases as well as hurts, because once we have an intimate relationship with a person, our souls' bond. This will cause further problems down the line when we meet our mate for life and marry. It is important to try and live a pure life and save it for the one that is meant for us in matrimony so that we don't bring baggage into that relationship. God is not trying to be mean here. He is trying to give you the best life has to offer in relationships with the opposite sex. One moment of pleasure outside this guideline is not worth the lifetime of regret that will follow.

Day 17. Isaiah 40:29-31
"He giveth power to the faint; and to them that have no might he increaseth strength. Even the youths shall faint and be weary, and the young men shall utterly fall: But they that wait upon the Lord shall renew their strength; they shall mount up with wings as eagles; they shall run, and not be weary; and they shall walk, and not faint."

Thought of the day: God doesn't always come when we want Him to, but He always comes on time. He will give us the power to hold on until He does come if we will trust Him. We need to learn to have patience in the waiting period. We will gain strength once we overcome, and it will teach us each time we do, that we can trust not only in God but in His divine timing also.

Day 18. 1 Samuel 15:23a
"For rebellion is as the sin of witchcraft, and stubbornness is as iniquity and idolatry."

Thought of the day: When we walk in disobedience, God is upset with us. He is not only upset because we are not obeying Him, but he is upset because it breaks our fellowship and blessings with God. Obedience is so important to God that He places that sin along with the sins we would normally fear and never do. Let's strive to please our Father in everything we do and say.

Day 19. Matthew 26:41
"Watch and pray, that ye enter not into temptation: the spirit indeed is willing, but the flesh is weak."

Thought of the day: In our busy lives, it is easy to get caught up in the world system. But we need to remember that we are not a part of this world. If we are not careful, it will drag us down to the pits and bondage just like the lost. We need to always take time to pray and listen to God's direction. We, in our human bodies, get tired. Why not try to pray and meditate on God first thing in the morning and then as much as you can throughout the day? That way, you at least will have given your best at the beginning instead of catch-up, after being tired at the end of the day. Remember, Satan is looking for those who he can devour.

Day 20. Jeremiah 1:4-5

"Then the word of the Lord came unto me, saying, Before I formed thee in the belly I knew thee; and before thou camest forth out of the womb I sanctified thee, and I ordained thee a prophet unto the nations."

Thought of the day: Although this verse is talking about a particular purpose, it also pertains to all of us. God is the one that gives life. It is from Him that we have our being; This is one of the reasons we should not abort our babies. It may have been a mistake in your life, or maybe even forced pregnancy on you, but God will have a purpose for that child if we go ahead and let it live. We never know what God's purpose is for that child. That child might be the answer to cancer or become our next great leader. He also has a plan for you. Are you working toward the plan that God has for you in your life? Ask Him today what He wants you to do and go out to fulfill your purpose in life.

Day 21. 2 Kings 22:1-2

"Josiah was eight years old when he began to reign, and he reigned thirty and one years in Jerusalem. And his mother's name was Jedidah, the daughter of Adaiah of Boscath. And he did that which was right in the sight of the Lord, and walked in all the way of David his father, and turned not aside to the right hand or to the left."

Thought of the day: Imagine what it must have been like to have a leader of your nation that was only eight years old. Yet at just eight years old, Josiah walked in the paths of God and led the nation in that direction. This was probably a result of things he was taught as a baby. The things we teach our children will stay with them throughout their lives. It is important to teach them the things of God so that they might not only stay in His way but lead others in that way as well. He was successful also because he allowed God to lead, and he followed. The Bible says, "If any man lack wisdom, let him ask of God, that giveth to all men liberally, and upbraideth not: and it shall be given him." James 1:5. Do you need wisdom in an area? Ask God, and He will give you the wisdom to make the right decision.

Day 22. Galatians 6:7-8
"Be not deceived; God is not mocked: for whatsoever a man soweth, that shall he also reap. For he that soweth to his flesh shall of the flesh reap corruption; but he that soweth to the Spirit shall of the Spirit reap life everlasting."

Thought of the day: Many people get the idea, that because God didn't strike them down when they committed a sin, they are getting away with it. God is full of patience and mercy; but if we continue to walk in disobedience, judgment will come. God is keeping a record of everything, even our idle words. Trust me; God knows what you are doing. Don't push Him to discipline you. He is a good Father, and He will do what is necessary to keep you out of trouble; even if it hurts Him to do so.

Day 23. James 1:2-4
"My brethren, count it all joy when ye fall into divers temptations; Knowing this, that the trying of your faith worketh patience. But let patience have her perfect work, that ye may be perfect and entire, wanting nothing."

Thought of the day: Does this mean that I should be happy when I am going through tough stuff or struggling to stay out of temptation? Not at all! Hard times are not a happy time for anyone in their right mind. But when we understand the end result, we can be joyful knowing that in the end, it will bring something valuable, and much needed in our lives or in the life of another. We have a God that knows the end from the beginning. Trust Him that He knows what He needs to accomplish during those hard times in your life and that He will help you to overcome temptations if you will allow Him to.

Day 24. 2 Corinthians 12:10
"Therefore, I take pleasure in infirmities, in reproaches, in necessities, in persecutions, in distresses for Christ's sake: for when I am weak, then am I strong."

Thought of the day: It is hard to be content when you are sick or going through hard times. But when we remember all Christ has done for us and the pain He endured, it should give us the strength to be willing to go through the things He is allowing. He has a purpose, even though we might not be able to understand that purpose at the moment. Ask for God's healing and overcoming power, but if you must walk through these hard times, pray for His strength to carry you through. The world watches us as we go through these things. They want to see how we hold up. If we stay with God, they will see God's awesome power in our situation no matter the outcome.

Day 25. 2 Corinthians 5:17
"Therefore, if any man be in Christ, he is a new creature: old things are passed away; behold, all things are become new."

Thought of the day: One of the true signs that you are saved; is your life should change to be more like Christ. The things you once enjoyed should now fade if they were sinful. People should be able to look at your life and know you are a Christian without you even mentioning it. Does your life show you have been born again? If not, maybe you need to check on your salvation.

Day 26. 1 Corinthians 15:57
"But thanks be to God, which giveth us the victory through our Lord Jesus Christ."

Thought of the day: If we are on the Lord's side, we will have victory, it may not be in this life, but we will have victory one way or another. When Christ said it was finished on the Cross, that covered everything we might face in this life. He became the Victor in ALL things.

Day 27. 1 Corinthians 15:58
"Therefore, my beloved brethren, be ye stedfast, unmoveable, always abounding in the work of the Lord, forasmuch as ye know that your labour is not in vain in the Lord."

Thought of the day: As Christ said when He was on Earth, He must be about the Father's business, we should be too. We should try our best every day to do all we can for the Kingdom of God. God, on the day of judgment, will give us our just reward for all that we do for Him. Because Christ did what He was sent to do, it made a difference in our life. We should do all we can do as well, so we can make a difference in others.

Day 28. 1 John 4:16
"And we have known and believed the love that God hath to us. God is love; and he that dwelleth in love dwelleth in God, and God in him."

Thought of the day: People often blame God as being this mean and unjust being that is just waiting to beat us over the head when we mess up. That kind of thinking comes from people who have never allowed God into their lives. Once a person allows God in their life, they soon see the goodness of God. The truth is, all that is bad and hurtful came from mankind when he disobeyed God in the beginning. God only had good intended for us, but we made the choice to rebel, and now we suffer the consequences of that action.

Day 29. Matthew 7:12
"Therefore, all things whatsoever ye would that men should do to you, do ye even so to them: for this is the law and the prophets."

Thought of the day: Here is where we get the "golden rule," but we are not just to do what others do to us. If others wrong us, we still shouldn't wrong them, but instead, be merciful and forgiving toward them. It is hard to do I know, but Christ has done it for us, and we should for others. When we act as Christ would act, He Himself will award our actions.

Overcoming Words for March

Chapter 4

Day 1. Mark 10:45
"For even the Son of man came not to be ministered unto, but to minister, and to give his life a ransom for many."

Thought of the day: As a Christian, we should make it our desire to serve others. Christ was willing to give up all His Glory and Power He held in Heaven, just to come down and serve man and to meet his most important need, his need of salvation. But He didn't stop with just that, but touched everyone He encountered; even knowing that one day, they would turn on Him and crucify Him. Have you been a help to someone lately? Try and find someone to minister to today.

Day 2. Matthew 6:2
"Therefore, when thou doest thine alms, do not sound a trumpet before thee, as the hypocrites do in the synagogues and in the streets, that they may have glory of men. Verily I say unto you, they have their reward."

Thought of the day: Have you ever seen someone go around telling everyone they see; about something they may have done to help someone else? Maybe they gave some money or helped them in a physical way. The way they act, they make it appear that the person they helped should serve them for the rest of their lives because of the act of kindness they bestowed upon the person in need. But a person with a servant's heart could care less about self-glory. We should not make a big deal when we do something good for others. As a matter of fact, when we try to get the praise, that is the reward we will get; just praise from men. But when we do it in secret, God will reward us openly. I would rather have God's praise than man. How about you?

Day 3. Jeremiah 12:1
"Righteous art thou, O Lord, when I plead with thee: yet let me talk with thee of thy judgments: Wherefore doth the way of the wicked prosper? wherefore are all they happy that deal very treacherously?"

Thought of the day: I am sure you at one time or another thought, how could that person being so evil, seem to get everything they want. We must remember, not all people are saved. If they are not saved, no matter what they obtain in this world, it is not worth losing their soul for eternity. If they don't change their standing with Christ, they will die and go to Hell for the rest of eternity. When we think of it that way, we should pity them knowing that the only joy they will have will be on this side of life. We believers, on the other hand, may not have it all here in this world, but we will have all this and more forever, once we reach our home God has prepared for us.

Day 4. Matthew 6:21
"For where your treasure is, there will your heart be also."

Thought of the day: This verse speaks for itself. Do you seem to want more of this world and its treasures, or do you want more of God and what He can offer? When you get to the bottom of that question, it will give you a good understanding of the relationship you have with God. Give yourself a check-up and see if you are in right standing with God. That is not to say that having earthly things is wrong; it just depends on the priority they have in your life and what you do with those treasures.

Day 5. John 11:35
"Jesus wept."

Thought of the day: It has always made me upset when I hear a parent tell a child not to cry when there is a reason to do so. Crying is a God-given emotion, and it is used to help us overcome hard times in our lives. Christ was the most powerful person that has lived and yet He felt the need to cry. Crying doesn't make you weak or a wimp. It shows you that you have emotions and are willing to show them. If you never cry, chances are your heart is hardened and that is a dangerous place to be.

Day 6. 1 Samuel 30:6
"And David was greatly distressed; for the people spake of stoning him, because the soul of all the people was grieved, every man for his sons and for his daughters: but David encouraged himself in the Lord his God."

Thought of the day: Sometimes in life, there is no one around to give you the encouragement you might need at the time. It may seem that the whole world is against you. It is in those times that we must draw on the good things and victories we had in the past and encourage ourselves, knowing this is just for a season and we will soon overcome.

Day 7. Matthew 9:36
"But when he saw the multitudes, he was moved with compassion on them, because they fainted, and were scattered abroad, as sheep having no shepherd."

Thought of the day: I am so grateful for Christ's compassion for man. Even after man crucified Him, He still shows compassion. All we have ever deserved was death, yet He continually shows us compassion and His desire to have fellowship with Him.

Day 8. Luke 12:6-7
"Are not five sparrows sold for two farthings, and not one of them is forgotten before God? But even the very hairs of your head are all numbered. Fear not therefore: ye are of more value than many sparrows."

Thought of the day: God is love, and God loves all of His creation. Yes, even you. You might think that you have done so much wrong that God would never care for you. But He cares for ALL of mankind, even more than any other thing He has created here on earth. You might think that God is too busy for you. But there again, He loves you so much and spends so much time with you, that He even counts the hair on your head each day. Most people lose about 100-125 hairs a day. I would say that is a lot of love to spend that much time counting each hair that falls from your head. Don't you?

Day 9. Matthew 7:7
"Ask, and it shall be given you; seek, and ye shall find; knock, and it shall be opened unto you:"

Thought of the day: Once again. A verse like this doesn't mean that you will get everything you ask for. There are things that must happen before you get what you ask of God. You must be in His Will. You must have the right motive in your asking. You must be walking in His direction. Even then, God may want something else for you. But more importantly, in this verse, it's not just asking, but it is putting action to your prayer. There are also the actions of seeking and knocking or looking for the open door of opportunities. God is not your genie just to do your bidding. He expects us to do our part too.

Day 10. Luke 6:38
"Give, and it shall be given unto you; good measure, pressed down, and shaken together, and running over, shall men give into your bosom. For with the same measure that ye mete withal it shall be measured to you again."

Thought of the day: Many people use this verse to hold God responsible to give them money when they give to God. First, for that to happen, you must give cheerfully and not with an alternative motive to get money. Frankly, this verse applies to everything in our life. If we give Love, Love will come back to us. If we give compassion, compassion will come back to us. If we give forgiveness, we will receive forgiveness. You will never out-give God, no matter what you are giving away.

Day 11. Matthew 26:40
"And he cometh unto the disciples, and findeth them asleep, and saith unto Peter, What, could ye not watch with me one hour? "

Thought of the day: I know we would all like to think that we would be there for Christ when He needs us. I've heard many say, "If I had been there the day that Christ was crucified, I would have taken up for Him." But the truth is, we are just like Peter and the rest. We are human, with human faults. We live in this sinful, imperfect body. We want to do right but often don't. Paul said he fought that battle daily and we do too. Even so, we should try to remember that Christ's work is completed through our hands and mouth. Let's try and remember all He did for us and how hard it must have been for Him to do so in this flesh and do our best to please Him.

Day 12. Mark 8:36
"For what shall it profit a man, if he shall gain the whole world, and lose his own soul?"

Thought of the day: The world looks at influential or rich people as people of importance. We work hard and give so much of our lives to obtain that status. Sadly, however, this life will soon pass, and you will not take what you have made or have the position you are in after you are gone. It is only trusting in Christ Jesus as your personal Savior, will you be able to enter Heaven. You can have all the world has to offer, but if you don't have Christ, it is worthless, and you will spend eternity in Hell.

Day 13. Romans 8:39
"Nor height, nor depth, nor any other creature, shall be able to separate us from the love of God, which is in Christ Jesus our Lord."

Thought of the day: I'm so glad that I don't have to hold on to make it to Heaven. I am also glad that my Salvation can't be taken away. The all-powerful God almighty is the one holding me and will keep me till the day of redemption. Don't trust in your power or the power of anyone else but Jesus Christ to carry you through to the end.

Day 14. Galatians 6:1
"Brethren, if a man be overtaken in a fault, ye which are spiritual, restore such an one in the spirit of meekness; considering thyself, lest thou also be tempted."

Thought of the day: I know of people who think they are really spiritual. They constantly talk about other's sins and how they will be punished. When they do this, it shows just how far they really are from God. God doesn't take pleasure in that. He is long-suffering and not willing that anyone perish. For the people who judge, they have forgotten just what a wretched person they were before Christ and how quick they could return to that type of person. If you are truly a follower of Christ, you will pray for the one that has fallen and have compassion. Then you will gently lead them back to the ways of the Lord without judgment or condemnation. So, the next time you hear someone who CLAIMS to be spiritual, spouting off at the mouth about other people and their sins; know that they have a form of Godliness but are not really as spiritual as they think but rather far from it.

Day 15. Hebrews 10:31
"It is a fearful thing to fall into the hands of the living God."

Thought of the day: Because God is not seen, we often forget just how powerful He is. He is the one that spoke the entire universe into existence. Even just one of His angels, who don't have any power compared to God, killed thousands of God's enemies in just one night. Let's never forget just how powerful our God is and not tempt Him to show His wrath toward us. Next time you forget how big God is, look around. Everything you see, hear, smell tastes or think is being controlled by Him.

Day 16. Matthew 15:8
"This people draweth nigh unto me with their mouth, and honoureth me with their lips; but their heart is far from me."

Thought of the day: Dad would often say, you can talk the talk, but can you walk the walk? God is not impressed at how well we can shout in church, how much we give in the offering, or how many works we do for Him. He looks on the heart and determines if you are surrendered to Him. Have you had a heart check-up lately?

Day 17. Luke 12:19-20

"And I will say to my soul, Soul, thou hast much goods laid up for many years; take thine ease, eat, drink, and be merry. But God said unto him, Thou fool, this night thy soul shall be required of thee: then whose shall those things be, which thou hast provided?"

Thought of the day: Agur wrote in Proverbs 30:8-9 "Remove far from me vanity and lies: give me neither poverty nor riches; feed me with food convenient for me: Lest I be full, and deny thee, and say, Who is the Lord? or lest I be poor, and steal, and take the name of my God in vain." It is easy if we are not careful, once we have made enough to live comfortably, to take God for granted. Then we begin to slip in our walk with God, and before you know it, we are far from Him. Remember number one, that it is God that has allowed you to do the things you do, and two, it is God that determines how long you live on earth. Always give God the glory and praise due Him for all He has given you. Be thankful and obedient to what God gives you, no matter if it much or little; so you won't have regrets when the time comes for you to depart this earth.

Day 18. Romans 3:4

"God forbid: yea, let God be true, but every man a liar; as it is written, That thou mightest be justified in thy sayings, and mightest overcome when thou art judged."

Thought of the day: In our society today, it is being pushed to be "Politically Correct." This will not work with God, however. If God says something is wrong, it doesn't matter what man thinks, it's wrong. God has set certain standards, and no matter what man says, we should accept that standard as truth. His statements trump man. To give an example, many are saying today; there are many ways to reach God. But God's Word tells us the only way to Him, is through His Son Jesus Christ. You can believe what you want, but the truth is, Jesus Christ is the only way to God, even if it is against the belief of the popular view. God's Word is FINAL. Instead of listening to what man says is moral or correct, read God's Word for the final decision.

Day 19. Isaiah 40:22
"It is he that sitteth upon the circle of the earth, and the inhabitants thereof are as grasshoppers; that stretcheth out the heavens as a curtain, and spreadeth them out as a tent to dwell in:"

Thought of the day: Scientist has long denied that the Bible is the truth, but rather a fantasy or made-up ideas. God has given us many tangible facts to contradict that in His Word. Here is one of the best. Written almost 4000 years ago, the Bible stated that the world was round. We didn't confirm that statement until 1611. We do not have to defend God's Word as fact. It will defend itself in most cases. In other things like our Salvation, it has to be taken in Faith. There are more manuscripts to prove the Word of God is truer than any other thing or person that has ever lived. You can take what God says to the Bank. Trust it at face value.

Day 20. 1 John 2:1
"My little children, these things write I unto you, that ye sin not. And if any man sin, we have an advocate with the Father, Jesus Christ the righteous:"

Thought of the day: As long as we live in the fleshly body, there is no way we can live a perfect life. There will be a day that we all will stand before the Judge of all. We have seen with our own eyes, if a person has the money to afford a great attorney, they often are set free even though guilty, or at least receive a light sentence. I am so glad that I have Jesus Christ as my attorney when I mess up to speak for me in the Court of God. Who better than the Son of the Judge to defend you in the time of need? He already paid the price for my action by His Blood. Do you have Christ as your attorney?

Day 21. Ephesians 4:30
"And grieve not the holy Spirit of God, whereby ye are sealed unto the day of redemption."

Thought of the day: One of the ways we grieve the Holy Spirit is by our disobedience and sin. Imagine how it must feel to the Holy Spirit, part of the same Godhead as God Himself, who can't even look upon sin to be in the middle of sin by our actions. Jesus Christ sent the Holy Spirit to teach and guide us. Jesus Himself said He would never leave us. That being said, when we sin, we make the Holy Spirit go through what we are doing. The Holy Spirit understands the great cost Christ paid for our salvation and freedom from sin. When we deliberately sin against God, we, in essence, are spitting in the face of God. Think of it this way. Say your own child, saved the life of another person's child with his own life. Later you hear that child talking bad about your child. How would that make you feel knowing that the child wouldn't even be living, had it not been for your child's life? Would it make you sad, maybe even angry? The way we act reflects how much we care about God's gift of His Son for us. Let's keep that in mind as we go about our daily lives.

Day 22. 1 Corinthians 6:20
"For ye are bought with a price: therefore, glorify God in your body, and in your spirit, which are God's."

Thought of the day: When you purchase something that you work for; it's yours to do with as you please. Although we have been given free will by God, if we have trusted His Son as our pardon of sin, then we have been bought with the price of Christ Blood. He then adopted us into the family of God. Our lives should show that we are King's kids, a part of a royal family. Let's don't disgrace the Name of Jesus by living a life like a common man.

Day 23. Romans 12:19
"Dearly beloved, avenge not yourselves, but rather give place unto wrath: for it is written, Vengeance is mine; I will repay, saith the Lord."

Thought of the day: It is only natural, to want to bring harm or hurt to someone who has hurt us. But as children of God, we should act differently. That doesn't help our feelings of wanting justice, however. If we try to bring justice ourselves, we normally only bring more trouble to all involved. We needn't worry. We are God's children. If someone does something to your child, I am sure you will do what you can to defend them. God is no different. He will take care of His kids and will bring the proper actions that only He can give that will bring the right kind of justice. Let God be your executioner of justice. He will do it in a way that will be best for all that is involved.

Day 24. Romans 1:16
"For I am not ashamed of the gospel of Christ: for it is the power of God unto salvation to every one that believeth; to the Jew first, and also to the Greek."

Thought of the day: Our nation was founded on Godly principles and beliefs. Today, however, people are trying to shame the believer and silence them. They are even trying to bring charges against the believers, for their Faith and trying to do what God says. We should never be ashamed. We have a right, even more so, an obligation to speak up for the Faith. God said if we are ashamed of Him on earth, He would be ashamed of us. I don't want Him ever to be ashamed of me. How about you?

Day 25. Luke 23:43
"And Jesus said unto him, Verily I say unto thee, today shalt thou be with me in paradise."

Thought of the day: These words were spoken to a common criminal. One that society had cast away and said he wasn't worth living. Yet Christ, in all His love, said to this man on the cross that was guilty of everything charged; "Today shalt thou be with me in paradise". Man may say you aren't worth anything, but God was willing to pay a great price for you. Trust Him today as your Savior and have worth through His Son Jesus Christ.

Day 26. Acts 16:31
"And they said, Believe on the Lord Jesus Christ, and thou shalt be saved, and thy house."

Thought of the day: One of the great promises that God has made is that if we accept His salvation plan by Jesus Christ Blood, that our household will be saved as well. Now we all still have free will. But if we teach and live our new life before our household, in time, the Holy Spirit should begin a work in them that will cause them to want what you have. If you have unsaved loved ones, keep trusting in the Lord that they eventually will come to Him for salvation. Just keep living the life in front of them so as not to turn them away from it.

Day 27. John 14:6
"Jesus saith unto him, I am the way, the truth, and the life: no man cometh unto the Father, but by me."

Thought of the day: As we stated earlier. No matter what man says. There is only one way and one Faith. It is through Jesus Christ. You must trust and believe in Jesus Christ to live with God throughout eternity. "What can wash away your sins? Nothing but the Blood of Jesus."

Day 28. Ephesians 2:8
"For by grace are ye saved through faith; and that not of yourselves: it is the gift of God:"

Thought of the day: There is nothing we can do to merit salvation. The price of the Sin debt was paid in full by Jesus Christ. This doesn't mean that we shouldn't try to live our lives holy. As a matter of fact, we are commanded to. However, none of our works come close to being enough to make it to Heaven. Our works are more of an outward testimony of our love and appreciation for what Christ has done for us.

Day 29. John 10:10
"The thief cometh not, but for to steal, and to kill, and to destroy I am come that they might have life, and that they might have it more abundantly."

Thought of the day: There are many people that view God as someone that doesn't want us to have anything, or any type, of fun. But that is not the case. He doesn't want us to have anything that will harm us in any way. That is why He has set standards for us to live by. The enemy, however, Satan himself, will give us anything we desire and will even tempt us to obtain it. But his main goal is to destroy us or our testimony. Don't fall for his tricks. He is not your friend. He doesn't have your best at heart as God does.

Day 30. Proverbs 18:21
"Death and life are in the power of the tongue: and they that love it shall eat the fruit thereof."

Thought of the day: Wars and Peace, Love and hate, all come about from just words. Our words can bring healing or harm. Our words can build or destroy. It is important for us to think before we speak and determine how your words will bring about a reaction. It has been said, that is why God gave us two ears and one mouth so that we will listen twice before speaking. Even God's Word tells us to be slow to speak. Once something has been said in anger or hate, it can never be taken back. Be careful what you say, knowing that what you say is very powerful.

Day 31. Psalm 51:5
"Behold, I was shapen in iniquity; and in sin did my mother conceive me."

Thought of the day: Because of man's sin in the garden, all mankind is born in sin. We will struggle trying to keep our sinful flesh down, but thanks be unto God, if we trust in Jesus Christ, He will not only forgive us of our sins, but also gives us the power to overcome the temptation of it.

Overcoming Words for April

Chapter 5

Day 1. Galatians 6:9
"And let us not be weary in well doing: for in due season we shall reap, if we faint not."

Thought of the day: Life is so full of things that must be done today and all at a very fast pace. We have to get up early to get dressed to be ready to head to work. Then work an 8-hour day only to come home to tend to the kids, chores, and eating. By the end of the day we are exhausted. But we still need to do our best at doing the work that God has called us to do. Often this is left on the sidelines because of all the other demands in life. We need to begin the day by doing God's work. Reading His Word, praying and asking Him to guide us on what He wants us to accomplish each day. He instructs us to put Him first, and everything else will fall in place. I know life is demanding, and we get tired, but we must do as Paul said and keep our eyes on the prize of the high calling, knowing that in the end, we will be rewarded greatly.

Day 2. Deuteronomy 31:6
"Be strong and of a good courage, fear not, nor be afraid of them: for the Lord thy God, he it is that doth go with thee; he will not fail thee, nor forsake thee."

Thought of the day: You might not feel like you are a strong person or one that could do much for the Kingdom of God. But the Bible lets us know, that everything we do for Him, can only be done through His power and His power alone. He has already promised He would never leave us. He also said that He would speak for us when we didn't know what to say. It is by His promises that we should be able to feel strong, encouraged and faithful in what He has for us to do. Stop looking at your own talents and abilities and focus on the fact that God is all-powerful, all-knowing, and will do what is needed to get it done through you, not by you.

Day 3. Philippians 4:8
"Finally, brethren, whatsoever things are true, whatsoever things are honest, whatsoever things are just, whatsoever things are pure, whatsoever things are lovely, whatsoever things are of good report; if there be any virtue, and if there be any praise, think on these things."

Thought of the day: If you watch the news or watch worldly movies and even conversations with friends; you will soon get discouraged. All around us is negativity and gossip. If we would instead focus on only the things that are true, honest, just, pure, lovely, and things that have a good ending; our lives would change for the better. It's not that we are blinded to the things around us when we do this; it is the fact that we belong to a different world and our values and thoughts should reflect our world and not this world. Try today to only focus on the good things and see how much better your day will become.

Day 4. Isaiah 55:8
"For my thoughts are not your thoughts, neither are your ways my ways, saith the Lord."

Thought of the day: When we look at circumstances in life, we view it through man's eyes. You go to a job interview and think you are not qualified. You might feel the need to move into a different state or even better, in the mission field, but we wonder how we would ever make it. When we look at things based on what we can do on our own, we most always will feel it impossible. But God sees the ending from the beginning and has all the power and resources needed to get the job done. He has a plan already made for our lives if we will just trust in it. The more you begin to let Him take control, the more you will see, that He can do the impossible. So, trust more in His promises and less on your abilities.

Day 5. Romans 6:23
"For the wages of sin is death; but the gift of God is eternal life through Jesus Christ our Lord."

Thought of the day: God had already told Adam and Eve what the punishment would be if they disobeyed (sinned). It would be both a physical death and a spiritual death, which is a separation from God for eternity. That punishment of Sin has been passed down to all mankind from that day forward. But God loved you and me so much that He made a way of escape. He gave His only Son to die in our stead if we would just trust in Him and accept that payment. It is not as the world portrays that God is sending people to Hell. It is each person's own choice to go to Hell. His love wants us all to be reconciled back to Him. Have you accepted His payment plan? If not, do it today.

Day 6. 1 John 5:13
"These things have I written unto you that believe on the name of the Son of God; that ye may know that ye have eternal life, and that ye may believe on the name of the Son of God."

Thought of the day: Do you ever struggle wondering if you are truly saved or not? I have seen many people confused if they really were saved or not. That is not only sad, but tormenting to the person that is struggling with that. But the good news is, you don't have to continue to wonder. You can truly know that you are born again. The reason most people have doubt is because they are basing their Faith on emotions or works or maybe even both. You can't do anything to be saved on your own power besides trusting in Christ Blood atonement and asking Him in your life. You won't always feel saved either. It is by Faith and Faith alone. Once you understand that, you can know that you are saved and will be until Christ calls you home. What a comfort in knowing that.

Day 7. Proverbs 18:22
"Whoso findeth a wife findeth a good thing, and obtaineth favour of the Lord."

Thought of the day: Wives get a poor rap and are often the mainline of jokes. People say things like, "I married to the ball and chains" or "this is my old lady." Wives are often portrayed in the negative. This may be caused because the man that married her didn't wait on God to send him the right one. If you do your part as a man, and let God do His part by sending you the right woman; you will find that she compliments everything in your life. I'm not saying that life will always be a bed of roses, but life will be much better when you have the right woman to share it with.

Day 8. 2 Timothy 1:7
"For God hath not given us the spirit of fear; but of power, and of love, and of a sound mind."

Thought of the day: Fear is not an attribute of a Christian. God is all-powerful and is full of love. We are His children, so we should have his characteristics. We keep a sound mind by prayer, Bible reading, and obedience. Fear will try at times to enter us to keep us from moving forward. But remember, that fear comes from the enemy. Keep marching. Keep moving. Walk-in victory, the power is within you in Christ Jesus.

Day 9. Hebrews 11:1
"Now faith is the substance of things hoped for, the evidence of things not seen."

Thought of the day: We are trained from a child to believe if we can't see it, it doesn't exist. But with God, we must walk in Faith, which is believing, although we can't see. With God, Faith is tangible. It is a substance, which to God, is His guarantee and assurance. Once what we had Faith in, comes into being, it then becomes the evidence or proof that the Faith was the underlining source of our obtaining whatever it was we were believing for. Walk-in Faith and the assurance that God will do what He says He will do.

Day 10. Romans 8:28
"And we know that all things work together for good to them that love God, to them who are the called according to his purpose.

Thought of the day: Have you ever gotten upset with God because you didn't get your way, or because a loved one you were praying for, died? There are many times in life that God seems He didn't answer our prayers. He is not so much concerned with what we want, but more so, on what is best for us. It reminds me of the story of Hezekiah on his death bed and asks God not to let him die. God honored that prayer and Hezekiah lived another 15 years. However, those were the worst years for Hezekiah than any time of his life. Like the old television show "Father knows best," God knows best. He is much greater than any earthly father and will never give us something that we don't need. When things don't seem to be going your way, remember, God WILL work it out for your good.

Day 11. Isaiah 54:17

"No weapon that is formed against thee shall prosper; and every tongue that shall rise against thee in judgment thou shalt condemn. This is the heritage of the servants of the Lord, and their righteousness is of me, saith the Lord."

Thought of the day: Satan doesn't use chemical weapons or weapons of mass destruction to defeat us. He uses subtle things. It might be a hurtful word from a friend or fear of something. It might be discouragement or even desire. It can be as simple as making our lives too busy to have time to read God's Word. But if we stand guard, trust God and follow Him, God will make sure that you will be on the winning side.

Day 12. 1 Peter 5:6

"Humble yourselves therefore under the mighty hand of God, that he may exalt you in due time."

Thought of the day: To me, one of the most obnoxious type persons is one who thinks they are better than anyone else. Christ too had a problem with such people. You will notice, Christ had more correction given to the Scribes and Pharisees than even a sinner. God hates a haughty spirit. It was that same haughty, prideful spirit that Satan had when God threw him out of Heaven. Instead, if you will be more of a servant, God will raise you up in position and power. He wants to get all the glory for what happens in your life. Be humble and allow God to advance you.

Day 13. Ecclesiastes 3:1

"To every thing there is a season, and a time to every purpose under the heaven:"

Thought of the day: Isn't it hard to wait for something good that you know is coming? Like children on Christmas morning waiting to open their gifts, we at times get anxious. But God is a God of order and timing. He has each step planned. If you haven't gotten that job promotion yet, or the spouse you are looking for, keep waiting and trusting. No matter what, it is all in the timing. That is why God said for us to be anxious for nothing. He's got this!!! Just wait and see! It is normally when we jump ahead of God when we get in trouble.

Day 14. Proverbs 27:17

"Iron sharpeneth iron; so a man sharpeneth the countenance of his friend."

Thought of the day: Many people, especially young and young adults, want to hang around the "cool" people. But as children of God, we are a cut above the rest. We have a higher calling and should hang with the people who have a higher purpose as well. It is when we hang with people that have that same calling, that we develop even greater in our lives. It's like if you want to be a pianist, then practice with another who is at least on your level or above. Then the two of you can learn from one another to be great at what you do. Don't settle for second best to fit in. Make your life count and be the best you can be. Vanity will fade, but determination and dedication will give great results as long as you live.

Day 15.   2 Corinthians 5:21
"For he hath made him to be sin for us, who knew no sin; that we might be made the righteousness of God in him."

Thought of the day: We often take what Christ did on the cross for us for granted. It is hard for our sinful flesh to understand the hurt and anguish it must have been for Christ, the one who had never sinned against His Father, to take on our Sin. Even now, the Holy Spirit grieves when we carry Him into our sinful nature. Let's try, even though we will never be perfect, to do the best we can to stay obedient to the Father. It cost Christ far more than we realize to buy our pardon. Let's show Him we care and appreciate what He has and is doing for us.

Day 16.   Matthew 23:27
"Woe unto you, scribes and Pharisees, hypocrites! for ye are like unto whited sepulchres, which indeed appear beautiful outward, but are within full of dead men's bones, and of all uncleanness."

Thought of the day: I know so many Christians who talk like they never sin. Always putting down others who do. But I can assure you, each and every one of them, have a sin within them that they fight with daily. We all do. It is part of our sinful, fleshly nature. God is not impressed with our outward actions. He judges our motivation. Our heart. Where is your heart with God today? Are you just giving lip service? Or are you being the servant He has called you to be in action.

Day 17. Matthew 19:14
"But Jesus said, Suffer little children, and forbid them not, to come unto me: for of such is the kingdom of heaven."

Thought of the day: I thank God, that He takes out the time for even the youngest person and will do something great for them in their life if they will allow Him. One of the ways that we must come to Him in a childlike state is our trust in Him. Think back when you were just a young child. Did you ever wonder if your dad was going to make enough money for the bills? Did you ever wonder where your next meal was coming from? Unless you lived with a person who didn't take care of you, I'm sure the answer would be no. As a child, we think our father can do anything, and we believe he will. God can, unlike men, do anything. We need to trust Him as we trusted our earthly father, that He will provide and take care of us. We are His children and is His delight in taking care of us.

Day 18. Proverbs 22:6
"Train up a child in the way he should go and when he is old, he will not depart from it."

Thought of the day: This verse has sometimes been taken wrong. Most believe that it means that if you train up a child in the Gospel of Christ, that later they would be saved if they go away from your teaching. Although I believe that will happen, the main thought here is the word "it" instead of "he." When we teach values and faith to our children, if they go on their own out in the world and do their own thing; as they get older, "it," (those teachings), will come back to their memory. That is why many times you hear children say they will never be like their parents. But as they grow older, they will say,

"Hum, I sounded just like my parents." They can run, but they can't hide from the real truth and values of Christ that were instilled in them at an early age. They may not be acting as they know it now, but in the future, no matter if they show it or not, it will be in their minds and hearts.

Day 19. Joshua 24:15
"And if it seem evil unto you to serve the Lord, choose you this day whom ye will serve; whether the gods which your fathers served that were on the other side of the flood, or the gods of the Amorites, in whose land ye dwell: but as for me and my house, we will serve the Lord."

Thought of the day: Every day that you live, every moment that you live; You are making a decision who you are going to serve. When Satan comes to tempt, and you yield, you have made the decision to follow him. If you resist, you made a decision to follow Christ. Be careful about all decisions you make, because, with each one, you are making a choice to follow God, or to follow Satan. Who are you serving today?

Day 20. Philippians 4:4
"Rejoice in the Lord always: and again I say, Rejoice."

Thought of the day: It's hard to rejoice when things are going wrong in our lives. But we can always rejoice because we know that our God is watching out for us and that He will do what is best for us in our lives eventually. So, give Him the praise now and walk in the victory, although you are in the midst of the storm. Joy comes in the morning.

Day 21. Proverbs 4:23
"Keep thy heart with all diligence; for out of it are the issues of life."

Thought of the day: You can tell a lot about a person by the things they say. Out of the abundance of the Heart, the Bible says, the mouth speaks. What is deep within us will always come out. That is why God looks on the heart to judge a person. It will always tell the truth of a person's life. David said to search his heart and see if there was any evil way in it and cleanse it if there was. We need to say the same prayer and keep our hearts pure for God.

Day 22. 2 Corinthians 10:4
"For the weapons of our warfare are not carnal, but mighty through God to the pulling down of strong holds;"

Thought of the day: We as believers, have two main weapons. The shield of Faith and the Word, which is the Sword of the Lord. But we also have an atomic bomb weapon. It is called prayer. Prayer unlocks the door to anything that we are facing in life. It can be activated at any moment or any emergency. Use your weapons to fight the enemy and stay victories in our battle for righteousness!

Day 23. Matthew 11:28
"Come unto me, all ye that labour and are heavy laden, and I will give you rest."

Thought of the day: Have life's trials gotten you down. That normally comes from us trying to deal with all of life's issues on our own. God never intended for us to do that. Yes, He does want us to do all we can, but He also wants us to rely on Him for the things that are too difficult for us to handle. Give God some of your load; He can handle it.

Day 24. Genesis 3:9
"And the Lord God called unto Adam, and said unto him, Where art thou?"

Thought of the day: Adam sinned against God and did just what we do today. He hid himself from God. You can't hide from God. God knew where Adam was. The question was for Adam to think where he was in his position with God. For Adam to think about what his actions have caused. Where are you? Are you trying to hide from God because of a sin or because you want to do your own thing? You can't hide. Might as well come closer to God so He can make things right that you have messed up.

Day 25. Proverbs 14:12
"There is a way which seemeth right unto a man, but the end thereof are the ways of death."

Thought of the day: You don't have to live in blatant sin to be trapped in something that later will make you wish you had done differently. Society teaches us certain things. One is that a man should work for his family. That is the truth. Man should work for his family. But a man shouldn't work so much, that he spends all of his time making money only to find at the end of life, he never took the time for his family or God. That would be the *death* of being able to redeem the time. Make sure you take the time to consult with God on all the decisions you are making so you can make sure you are making the right ones; Not decisions that will leave you in the dark.

Day 26. Malachi 3:10
"Bring ye all the tithes into the storehouse, that there may be meat in mine house, and prove me now herewith, saith the Lord of hosts, if I will not open you the windows of heaven, and pour you out a blessing, that there shall not be room enough to receive it."

Thought of the day: God commanded that we bring the tithes, all of it, to His house. But, for many churches, they shouldn't be getting all the tithe. Many churches are spending God's money on making the building beautiful and investing in lights and all kinds of entertainment that God didn't call them to do. This may not be so wrong in itself. I believe God's house should be nice. But if it is taking away from what God said to use it for, it becomes wrong. He said to give the tithe so there could be meat in His house. He tells us to feed the hungry and take care of the widow. The church also needs resources and to support missionaries. Plant your tithes in fertile ground so the Kingdom of God, not the Kingdom of Man can benefit. If you do that, you will never out-give God.

Day 27. Romans 12:14
"Bless them, which persecute you: bless, and curse not."

Thought of the day: WOW! Now that is a hard statement. Our flesh wants to have the last word. Our flesh wants to make people pay when they do us wrong. Our flesh wants us to gossip to everyone about the person that did us wrong. But God, wants us to show Mercy as He has shown us Mercy. When we remember how we should have been treated by God, then it might just be easier for us to show Mercy for those that have wronged us.

Day 28. Jeremiah 33:3
"Call unto me, and I will answer thee, and show thee great and mighty things, which thou knowest not."

Thought of the day: Often, God is the last person we talk to when we get ourselves in trouble. He is waiting to give us the direction if we will call on Him. And what's even greater, is that He is awake at any hour of the day to answer. We should go to Him first, and maybe we won't find ourselves in so many problems that we face when we don't. He has great things in store for us, if we will just ask.

Day 29. 1 Corinthians 1:27
"But God hath chosen the foolish things of the world to confound the wise; and God hath chosen the weak things of the world to confound the things which are mighty;"

Thought of the day: Man prides himself on his own intellect. We hold our chest out and think we have all the world's answers. We think we know how the earth was formed. We think we know about life. But it seems, the more intelligent a person is, the more stupid he becomes. God said the earth, and everything was formed by Him just by saying the word. Simple, right? God said we need to be saved and to do that, all we have to do is believe and trust in Christ Jesus and His Blood. Simple, right? God said He made man out of the dust of the earth and breathe life into him. Simple, right? But, man in all his knowledge, can't accept that all this is done without his help or understanding. The Bible says that even the Gospel is foolish to those that don't believe. They say we just believe in God because we are weak and need a crutch. I believe in God because I know He exists. I talk to Him daily. He answers my prayers. He lives inside of me. I didn't come from a monkey. The world was created with the big bang, but the bang was God speaking. However, all of these so-called intelligent people, will one day believe God. Unfortunately, it will be too late. But at that time, they will still bow before Him and proclaim Him King. It is a fool that says there is no God. The Bible says that even the devils believe and tremble. Do you believe?

Day 30. John 9:4
"I must work the works of him that sent me, while it is day: the night cometh, when no man can work."

Thought of the day: Christ, although equal with God, knew the importance of not only working for God but doing all He could while He had the time to do it. What are you doing with your time? Are you giving God your best years or are you waiting till you are about to depart this world to start working for Him? If Christ thought it important to give it His all and do it first; Don't you think you should too?

Overcoming Words for May

Chapter 6

Day 1. Romans 10:9-10
"That if thou shalt confess with thy mouth the Lord Jesus, and shalt believe in thine heart that God hath raised him from the dead, thou shalt be saved. For with the heart man believeth unto righteousness; and with the mouth confession is made unto salvation."

Thought of the day: God wants us to have fellowship restored with Him after the fall of man in the garden so much, that He made a plan of Salvation so simple, that even a child could understand. All we must do is to understand and agree that Jesus Christ is Lord. Also, believe He is the Son of God and was raised from the dead and ask him to come into our lives. That's it! But there is one important step. This act, in essence, is an agreement that we need Him, and we acknowledge our sinful nature. But the important step is not just believing it and confessing it; but it must be done with our heart, not just our mind. We must truly be repentant and want Christ in. If you do that, then He has promised He would forgive you of your sins and take you in as His own. What a great God we serve!

Day 2. Matthew 22:37-39
"Jesus said unto him, Thou shalt love the Lord thy God with all thy heart, and with all thy soul, and with all thy mind.
This is the first and great commandment. And the second is like unto it, Thou shalt love thy neighbour as thyself."

Thought of the day: In the Old Testament, there were over 600 things a person had to do, not including the ten commandments, to be in the right fellowship with God. After Christ death, those all were done away with, and now there are only two commandments we must follow. To love God with all our hearts and to love others. This sounds simple, right? But when you really look into what is involved in having real love for God and mankind; it goes pretty deep. Love will tolerate much, forgive much and cover much. It is so much to it that Christ said that ALL of the other laws hinge on just these two laws. If we do just those two, we won't desire to steal, kill, hurt our brother or sister. We will only want to do what is just and right. How is your LOVE life?

Day 3. Hebrews 4:12
"For the word of God is quick, and powerful, and sharper than any two-edged sword, piercing even to the dividing asunder of soul and spirit, and of the joints and marrow, and is a discerner of the thoughts and intents of the heart."

Thought of the day: The Word of God is so powerful that it can take the meanest, cold, heartless man and change him into a gentle caring person. It can bring healing to the body, peace to the soul and guidance to the lost. It can give answers to life's most hidden questions. The Word of God is the most powerful weapon we have. Sadly, many don't ever pick it up to read it. How often do you read God's Word? Try and make it a daily thing and your life will change for the better.

Day 4. Acts 1:8
"But ye shall receive power, after that the Holy Ghost is come upon you: and ye shall be witnesses unto me both in Jerusalem, and in all Judaea, and in Samaria, and unto the uttermost part of the earth."

Thought of the day: Often many believers focus on the power of the Holy Spirit, meaning they will be able to cast out demons, heal the sick and raise the dead. But here, it plainly says that we will have power to witness about God to everyone. I believe that God can give us power through Jesus Christ to do all of the other things mentioned when He wants to use us for that, but we should be more focused on winning the lost to Christ. That is our great commission and what we have been called to do. Are you doing your part to let others know there is a Hell to avoid and a Heaven to gain?

Day 5. Proverbs 15:1
"A soft answer turneth away wrath: but grievous words stir up anger."

Thought of the day: If you ever want to see this is a perfect example, watch a married couple that have a disagreement. Most will yell and fuss, trying to prove to the others that they are right. If you have been married any length of time, I'm sure you can relate. But the next time you find yourself in that position and words are flying, stop and calmly say, "I love you, and I'm sorry." It's hard to stay mad after you hear words like that spoken to you. You will be amazed at how that gentleness will drive away all the tension in the room. We have been instructed by God to try and live peaceably with all men. Start today.

Day 6. Psalm 19:1
"The heavens declare the glory of God; and the firmament sheweth his handywork."

Thought of the day: I never will understand how a person can't believe there is a God. When I stop and watch the mighty ocean waves crash upon the beach to a certain point and then return. Or when I see the countless stars on a moonless night. Or even watch a colony of ants goes about doing their job; it lets me know there must be a Divine Creator. God's power is made known through His creation even to the people who have never heard of His name. "When I consider thy heavens, the work of thy fingers, the moon, and the stars, which thou hast ordained; What is man, that thou art mindful of him? And the son of man, that thou visitest him?" Psalm 8:3-4

Day 7. 1 Corinthians 13:13
"And now abideth faith, hope, charity, these three; but the greatest of these is charity."

Thought of the day: Many people have the blessed hope and faith in our Lord Jesus Christ. But I wonder how many of those same people have the love that God wants us to have toward Him and others. The Bible says that God is love. If we are His children, then we should be showing love. Paul went on to say before this, a list of things that we could do and all were admirable and needful, but according to this verse, love trumps most everything else. Are you abiding in love? Sometimes it is easier to give or help people, than to love them when they are unlovable. God does it for us; let 's do it for Him.

Day 8. Matthew 28:19-20
"Go ye therefore, and teach all nations, baptizing them in the name of the Father, and of the Son, and of the Holy Ghost: Teaching them to observe all things whatsoever I have commanded you: and, lo, I am with you always, even unto the end of the world. Amen."

Thought of the day: This is part of the Great Commission we are to be doing, which is to go out and tell everyone we can about Christ and His Salvation. Many churches and saints of God do a great job of that. Where we often fail, however, is to not only share with them the Gospel, but to train and follow-up with them to make them disciples so they can be strong in their newfound Faith. Let's not forget to help them grow once they accept Christ, lest they be overcome and fall back into their sin.

Day 9. 1 Peter 5:8
"Be sober, be vigilant; because your adversary the devil, as a roaring lion, walketh about, seeking whom he may devour:"

Thought of the day: Make no mistake about it, Satan is not your friend. He is waiting and watching for that weak moment in your life where he can get a foothold in to discourage, tempt, and defeat you in any way he can. Keep a watchful eye. Stay alert. Stay near the flock and God. Like a lion, once he singles you out, he has a better chance of defeating you.

Day 10. Isaiah 26:3
"Thou wilt keep him in perfect peace, whose mind is stayed on thee: because he trusteth in thee."

Thought of the day: I have seen many people in my ministry fretting about so much in life, even though they claim to be Christians. Almost always, when I dig into their lives a little, I find that they spend very little time praying, reading the Bible or attending Church. To be victories in life, we must do all of the above. We must go through things, with the Faith we have been taught, by doing so, we can see how God delivers us out. We will begin to understand; God will always make a way for us. We must walk and talk with Him daily, not just when we find ourselves in a mess, to have peace, in the midst of the storm.

Day 11. 1 Corinthians 2:9
"But as it is written, Eye hath not seen, nor ear heard, neither have entered into the heart of man, the things which God hath prepared for them that love him."

Thought of the day: I have been to many places in this world and have been awestruck with the beauty I've seen. The first time I saw the ocean or when I went to Ruby Falls, and they turned the lights on to that beautiful waterfall going through the mountain. Countless of sights come to my mind. But nothing, I mean nothing, this world has, can ever compare to what God has. John tried to tell what he saw, but even he said it was no way to put it into words nor could our minds conceive it. Living for Christ can get hard, but keep focused. There is coming a day when it will all be worth every mile.

Day 12. James 5:16

"Confess your faults one to another, and pray one for another, that ye may be healed. The effectual fervent prayer of a righteous man availeth much."

Thought of the day: I bet you don't know many people who confess their sins to others, do you? I can see why. Most people, when they hear a confession, can't wait to tell others what they heard. But if they are truly living a Christian lifestyle, instead of talking about it to others, they would try to keep it covered in love, prayer, and guidance. How does confession bring healing? When we confess our sin and expose ourselves, we free ourselves from the enemy telling us if anyone found out about our sin, we would be finished. It also opens us up to accountability in our lives with the one we confess to. Accountability is important in the life of a believer. If you can find that one person you can confess with confidence that they will do and act the way Christ commanded; Then the two of you will have a powerful relationship and an awesome effective prayer life. But I warn again, be careful who you choose to confess to, remember, we are all human and can fail. But I pity the man who will expose what has been privately confessed to him to another.

Day 13. Proverbs 16:18

"Pride goeth before destruction, and an haughty spirit before a fall."

Thought of the day: Be careful boasting of things you will or have done. God doesn't like a prideful spirit. I remember a story of a man who was wealthy. He had a dog and was going to take a trip. As he was boarding with his dog, the person in charge said the man would not be allowed to carry the dog in with him, but the dog had to go to the storage compartment for animals. The man threw a fit and boasted, "I am rich. I can buy my own boat. I can hire my own Captain. No one, not even God Himself can stop me." On the day of his departure, he was taking a shower, and the people in the home heard a loud noise in the bath where he was taking a shower. They continued to call out his name without a response from him. They opened the door and found him dead on the floor. When the doctors examined him, they said his heart had exploded from the inside out. I truly believe he signed his death sentence when he boasted that not even God could stop him. Anything we do in life is always done by the power of God and not ourselves. Remember that the next time you feel you are the one who has made you who you are.

Day 14. Romans 5:8
"But God commendeth his love toward us, in that, while we were yet sinners, Christ died for us."

Thought of the day: I love this verse. It's easy to love people that love us. But when they are hard to be around, it's hard to love them. Yet, Christ loved us in our sins. He loved us when we would talk bad about Him or make fun of Him and His followers. He loves us even after we are saved and are hard to live with or being disobedient. He proved the amount of His love by giving His life for ours. We did nothing to deserve that kind of love. Do you love Him enough to live your life for Him?

Day 15. Galatians 5:22-23
"But the fruit of the Spirit is love, joy, peace, long-suffering, gentleness, goodness, faith, Meekness, temperance: against such there is no law."

Thought of the day: There are Christians that claim they are filled with the Holy Ghost. They believe the proof is in their power. Many of these same believers have the meanest spirit. They constantly put others down and judge others' lives. If they are truly filled with the Holy Spirit, it will come out in the ways mentioned above. You won't need to tell others you are filled; it will show. Spend a little time looking over each of these attributes and see how they compare with your life. They will be your guide on how full you are of the Holy Spirit, not by how many works you do.

Day 16. Proverbs 17:17
"A friend loveth at all times, and a brother is born for adversity."

Thought of the day: Have you ever heard the term "fair-weathered friend"? That is the term used for a person who is only your friend when things are going well. It's hard to find a friend that will be with you even in the tough times. But I have good news. Jesus said He would never leave you and would be with you till the end. If you find yourself in need of a friend, call on Him. He will answer.

Day 17. Genesis 6:8
"But Noah found grace in the eyes of the Lord."

Thought of the day: You might wonder what Noah did to be picked to escape the destruction of the world. Short answer, we may never know the life he lived; but I can tell you the word Grace means unmerited or undeserved favor of God. If you have been saved from the flames of Hell, you have been saved by God's unmerited favor. There is nothing you did; it's all what He did. I can promise you, that Noah made it the same way; through God's Grace and Mercy alone.

Day 18. Romans 8:1
"There is therefore now no condemnation to them which are in Christ Jesus, who walk not after the flesh, but after the Spirit."

Thought of the day: Have you ever felt bad about yourself after you have committed a sin and hear a voice saying things like, "you are worthless," "you will never overcome this addiction." That voice isn't from God. God never condemns us. He will convict us before we commit a sin, telling us it is wrong or not to do it. But God will never condemn.

Day 19. Isaiah 53:4-5

"Surely he hath borne our griefs, and carried our sorrows: yet we did esteem him stricken, smitten of God, and afflicted. But he was wounded for our transgressions, he was bruised for our iniquities: the chastisement of our peace was upon him; and with his stripes we are healed."

Thought of the day: Don't ever listen to the majority of the world's opinion of God being a hater. Take the time and read Isaiah 53 along with the Gospels, and see all that Christ went through for us; knowing that it was all because of things we had done. We deserved death, but God loved us so much, that He took his vengeful anger against our sins on His only Son to spare us of His wrath. I don't know of anyone else who would have ever done that for someone who didn't deserve it. Do you? Oh, what love, the Father has bestowed on us.

Day 20. Matthew 16:26

"For what is a man profited, if he shall gain the whole world, and lose his own soul? or what shall a man give in exchange for his soul?"

Thought of the day: Would you be willing to go to a burning Hell for eternity in order to win a 500-billion-dollar lotto while living on earth? That would be foolish. But people do it for far less every day. They want to do what they want to do, not knowing or either not caring, what the cost is going to be. Christ offers abundant life, not only here, but also a life of eternity free of debt, pain, death, and so much more, just by believing in Him and doing His will. What are you trading your eternal soul for?

Day 21. Philippians 1:6
"Being confident of this very thing, that he which hath begun a good work in you will perform it until the day of Jesus Christ."

Thought of the day: If today, you find yourself in a situation that seems it will never come to an end; encourage yourself with this verse. It is not by your power and strength that your battles will be won. It's is by the all-powerful God that it will be completed if it is in the Father's Will that it be done at all. If it is not in His Will, He will give you the strength to bear the path that follows.

Day 22. Ephesians 6:10-11
"Finally, my brethren, be strong in the Lord, and in the power of his might. Put on the whole armour of God, that ye may be able to stand against the wiles of the devil."

Thought of the day: The verses that follow these describe the whole armor that we should wear. When you are in a battle, you need to have ALL of it for your safety and your advancement. Are you leaving a piece off? If so, you are in danger of getting hurt by the enemy. Every day put on your armor and be a victories fighter in life. By the way, the only part that is not covered, is the back. Why? Because God never wants us to run from the battle, but face it head-on.

Day 23. Matthew 6:24
"No man can serve two masters: for either he will hate the one, and love the other; or else he will hold to the one, and despise the other. Ye cannot serve God and mammon."

Thought of the day: The word despise is a hard word. The definition is; to regard as negligible, worthless, loath scorn, or distasteful. You would never use that word on how you feel about Christ, right? Well, every time that we decide to do what Satan says instead of Christ, we in all reality are making the choice to despise Christ and His Will. If we are going to serve Him, let's go all the way!

Day 24. Luke 9:35
"And there came a voice out of the cloud, saying, This is my beloved Son: hear him."

Thought of the day: God wanted the world to know who His Son was. Christ wants the world to know that we are God's children also made possible by Him. Christ always did the Will of His Father and never shamed His name. Can we say the same about us, as the world looks at you as God's child?

Day 25. Proverbs 14:34
"Righteousness exalteth a nation: but sin is a reproach to any people."

Thought of the day: You can see it in history. When our nation followed God, our nation was blessed. You can see it in yourself as well. When you follow God, your life is blessed. Sin has a payment of not only death but of hurt, pain, and destruction as well. The choice is yours.

Day 26. 1 Timothy 6:10
"For the love of money is the root of all evil: which while some coveted after, they have erred from the faith, and pierced themselves through with many sorrows."

Thought of the day: Money doesn't buy happiness, but God is not blinded about the need for it. In another place of the Word of God, it says that "money answereth all things." God knows that if we have money, we can afford food, shelter, health care and other necessities. He is not against us having money. It is when we love money, more than Him that He has a problem. Never let money overcome your walk with God. Money can bring you to a place of comfort or a place of ruin. It is all in how you treat it.

Day 27. Joshua 1:8
"This book of the law shall not depart out of thy mouth; but thou shalt meditate therein day and night, that thou mayest observe to do according to all that is written therein: for then thou shalt make thy way prosperous, and then thou shalt have good success."

Thought of the day: God's Word, besides the Blood of Christ, is the most important thing you can have. It is literally a blueprint on how to live life. It tells us how to eat so we can stay healthy, how to make good decisions so life will go smoother and even how to die so that we can live in peace for eternity. Read it daily, but more so, do what it says, and your life will change for the good.

Day 28. Romans 3:23
"For all have sinned, and come short of the glory of God;"

Thought of the day: For all my Super Spiritual, non-sinning friends out there. This verse is for you!!! You are not as great as you think you are. You can't see the condition you are in. We ALL have sinned and do so daily! Yes, even you! But thank God, that He is full of Mercy and Grace, that He sent His perfect, sinless Son to die in our stead so that we can live victorious over sin through Him.

Day 29. Deuteronomy 28:13
"And the Lord shall make thee the head, and not the tail; and thou shalt be above only, and thou shalt not be beneath; if that thou hearken unto the commandments of the Lord thy God, which I command thee this day, to observe and to do them:"

Thought of the day: People may try to lie about you or destroy your life. But you have this confidence; that in the end, God will never allow them to destroy you. What was meant for evil by them, will turn out good for you, IF you are obedient to God.

Day 30. 2 Timothy 2:15
"Study to shew thyself approved unto God, a workman that needeth not to be ashamed, rightly dividing the word of truth."

Thought of the day: It is not only reading the Word of God but studying it as well. You can take any verse and make it say what you want it to say. But if we keep it in context with the rest of the story, we will not twist its meaning. This is why there are so many denominations and false teachers. They are reading the Word, but not studying it or the historical background and who it is written to. Be a good student of God and STUDY so you will have the right answers on the test days in life.

Day 31. Galatians 2:20
"I am crucified with Christ: nevertheless I live; yet not I, but Christ liveth in me: and the life which I now live in the flesh I live by the faith of the Son of God, who loved me, and gave himself for me. "

Thought of the day: The Sin debt that we all had was paid by Christ's death on the cross. All Christ asks of us is to Crucify our fleshly desires. He doesn't want us to die a physical death for our Sin; He wants us to live against the fleshly desires. This is not something that we should hate, because everything He wants us to crucify, are things that will harm us. So why is that so hard for us to do at times? Are you living a crucified life for Christ?

Overcoming Words for June

Chapter 7

Day 1. Isaiah 53:6
"All we like sheep have gone astray; we have turned every one to his own way; and the Lord hath laid on him the iniquity of us all."

Thought of the day: ALL! I love that word. I know too many people who believe they never sin. We live in the flesh, and the effect of that is, we sometimes give in to the flesh. But thanks be to God, that He already had a plan for that. Jesus Christ, not only took care of my sins on the cross in my past, but also my present and future sins are covered too. That doesn't give me the right to sin, but I am covered when I do.

Day 2. Genesis 1:27
"So God created man in his own image, in the image of God created he him; male and female created he them."

Thought of the day: We have been created with a body, soul, and spirit. God is God the Father, God the Son and God the Holy Ghost. We might not look completely like what God looks like, but we should have enough of His attributes to be identified as His. Can people tell that you are the IMAGE of God? Christ said, if you have seen me, you have seen the Father. Our lives should be the same for people who look at us. Strive to be more than just the created image He created everyone to be, but strive to be more of His nature image as well.

Day 3. Hebrews 11:6
"But without faith it is impossible to please him: for he that cometh to God must believe that he is, and that he is a rewarder of them that diligently seek him."

Thought of the day: Faith; it is the assurance of our belief that God is who He says He is and will do what He says He will do. We must believe that, for us to receive from God. Our Salvation, our desires, everything about us will come only by the Faith we have in Him.

Day 4. Psalm 1:1
"Blessed is the man that walketh not in the counsel of the ungodly, nor standeth in the way of sinners, nor sitteth in the seat of the scornful."

Thought of the day: We are to be different from the world. We need to be an example to all who view our lives. We should never be doing things that might cause people to turn away from Christ. We need to be separate from the world and the things it does, but we also need to be around the world to give them the light of Christ. Balance it carefully because the world can get into us if we are not careful.

Day 5. Matthew 28:6
"He is not here: for he is risen, as he said. Come, see the place where the Lord lay."

Thought of the day: Christ dying for our sins is something to thank Him for always! But, had He not come up from the grave, His death would be meaningless. Thank God, Christ not only died but had the power to raise Himself up to offer His sacrifice for our sins to God. "He lives! He lives! Christ Jesus lives today!

Day 6. Mark 16:7
"But go your way, tell his disciples and Peter that he goeth before you into Galilee: there shall ye see him, as he said unto you."

Thought of the day: Have you ever felt you have disappointed the Lord so much that He would never want you again? Peter did. He even went as far as cursing and saying he never knew of Jesus. I'm sure that left Peter feeling useless and that Christ would disown him. I believe that is why Jesus said specifically when He rose again, go tell Peter also that had risen. He wanted Peter to know that all was forgiven, and He wanted to have fellowship with Him again. You have not out sinned God's Grace and Mercy. He desires fellowship with you again also. Just come to Him. He's calling for you.

Day 7. John 13:35
"By this shall all men know that ye are my disciples, if ye have love one to another."

Thought of the day: The biggest sign of your being saved, is love for another. We should love even people who don't do right. It doesn't mean we have to hang out with them, but we should care and pray for them. Is there love in your heart for those in your life? It is not a suggestion; it's a commandment.

Day 8. Psalm 8:3-4
"When I consider thy heavens, the work of thy fingers, the moon and the stars, which thou hast ordained; What is man, that thou art mindful of him? and the son of man, that thou visitest him?"

Thought of the day: Have you ever sat under the stars and looked at all that God has created? It's overwhelming. And He keeps all of it going all at once. Yet, He still has time to help us in the time of our need. What makes Him care for mankind so much, I can't explain, but I sure am glad He does.

Day 9. Romans 8:38-39
"For I am persuaded, that neither death, nor life, nor angels, nor principalities, nor powers, nor things present, nor things to come, Nor height, nor depth, nor any other creature, shall be able to separate us from the love of God, which is in Christ Jesus our Lord."

Thought of the day: There is nothing that will cause God to hate you. If you are His child, He will always love and care for you. There is also nothing in life that can pull Him away from you, not even Satan himself. Isn't that a comforting thought?

Day 10. 1 Thessalonians 5:16-18
"Rejoice evermore. Pray without ceasing. In everything give thanks: for this is the will of God in Christ Jesus concerning you." He is worthy of our praise. He deserves to hear from us. And we should give Him thanks for all He does.

Thought of the day: This is a good way to live. It is pretty straight forward. Rejoice, pray, and give thanks. That should be the daily actions of a believer.

Day 11. Job 14:1
"Man that is born of a woman is of few days and full of trouble."

Thought of the day: From the moment that we are born, there is a cry. I am sure you have experienced that every time everything seems to be going great, out of nowhere comes some unexpected trouble. God never intended this to be. He had designed us to live in a perfect world under perfect conditions. But we decided we wanted more. Our pride caused us to sin against God, which brought on the curse. But I am thankful that the story doesn't stop there. He also made a way of escape to where I can once again be in a perfect place under perfect conditions. All I have to do is accept Christ and repent and I can spend eternity in Heaven. You have that choice too. Will you allow your pride to keep you in the curse, or will you choose to be free?

Day 12. Isaiah 55:10-11

"For as the rain cometh down, and the snow from heaven, and returneth not thither, but watereth the earth, and maketh it bring forth and bud, that it may give seed to the sower, and bread to the eater: So shall my word be that goeth forth out of my mouth: it shall not return unto me void, but it shall accomplish that which I please, and it shall prosper in the thing whereto I sent it."

Thought of the day: When we speak the Word, no matter who we tell or if they receive it or not; it will always do what it was made to do. You might ask, "but what if a person you share the Word with doesn't accept Christ? Did the Word fail?" No, not at all. It was planted in their soul, and it will grow and keep reminding them they need to repent. The Word will always accomplish what it is sent to do.

Day 13. Proverbs 31:30

"Favour is deceitful, and beauty is vain: but a woman that feareth the Lord, she shall be praised."

Thought of the day: Don't EVER marry a woman because of her beauty. In time, we all will lose our beauty and looks as far as outward appearances. It is better to make sure they are beautiful on the inside. If they have enough inward beauty, it will begin to show on the outside too and make them appear beautiful.

Day 14. Psalm 19:14
"Let the words of my mouth, and the meditation of my heart, be acceptable in thy sight, O Lord, my strength, and my redeemer."

Thought of the day: It is only through the strength of God, that we can be acceptable in God's sight. He gives us the power to overcome the enemy. But the choice is still ours. Are you living in the power He has given to be acceptable in His sight? Is your lifestyle acceptable?

Day 15. John 14:1-3
"Let not your heart be troubled: ye believe in God, believe also in me. In my Father's house are many mansions: if it were not so, I would have told you. I go to prepare a place for you. And if I go and prepare a place for you, I will come again, and receive you unto myself; that where I am, there ye may be also."

Thought of the day: When life seems too much to bear, it is good to focus on what all, the Bible tells us that awaits us, when we get to Heaven. We have to remember; we are just passing through this life on our way to our eternal home. This world is not our home. The road gets hard, but keep focused on your destiny, not the journey.

Day 16. Psalm 139:14
"I will praise thee; for I am fearfully and wonderfully made: marvellous are thy works; and that my soul knoweth right well."

Thought of the day: Have you ever watched "The Miracle of Life" by Nova? If you haven't, you should. God spoke everything else into existence, but He took the time to create man. He created us to have fellowship with Him and bring Him glory. Let's make sure we are doing just that.

Day 17. Psalm 14:1
"The fool hath said in his heart, There is no God. They are corrupt, they have done abominable works, there is none that doeth good."

Thought of the day: To me, if a person looks at everything that is in the world and how it functions; you would be a fool not to think there is a creator somewhere keeping all this together. But not believing God is the creator is not near as serious, as not believing that He is the only way to Salvation. To not believe that, is definitely a fool!

Day 18. Psalm 34:18
"The Lord is nigh unto them that are of a broken heart; and saveth such as be of a contrite spirit."

Thought of the day: It is my opinion, that when we go through something that brings us hurt or pain and we cry out to God, but seems He is a million miles away; it is then, that He is just holding us. I know when people have a death, most can't even remember who came to visit. Those times in life are too hard to receive much more than comfort. God knows that, and He will carry you through but may do so in silence.

Day 19. Psalm 84:10
"For a day in thy courts is better than a thousand. I had rather be a doorkeeper in the house of my God, than to dwell in the tents of wickedness."

Thought of the day: What God has prepared for His saints, is so great, that even a street sweeper or toilet cleaner there, will be so much greater than anything this world has to offer. You don't want to miss that. This world has no eternal or lasting value. Only God can give us those things.

Day 20. John 15:13
"Greater love hath no man than this, that a man lay down his life for his friends."

Thought of the day: The ultimate sacrifice of another is to give your life. Our soldiers and emergency responders do this for the love of our country and their families. Christ gave His life so that we can live in freedom both here and in the hereafter. He gave the ultimate, so we don't have to. Let's live our lives in a way that shows Him how much we appreciate what He did for us.

Day 21. 2 Corinthians 12:9
"And he said unto me, My grace is sufficient for thee: for my strength is made perfect in weakness. Most gladly therefore will I rather glory in my infirmities, that the power of Christ may rest upon me."

Thought of the day: Paul wanted to serve God with everything he had and the best way possible. There was something in his life, however, that was giving him trouble. We don't know if it was physical, mental or spiritual, but something was upsetting him because he couldn't get rid of it. He prayed for God to take it, but God wouldn't. Why? Maybe because if Paul was delivered from it, he might become boastful of all he did. Regardless of why God didn't heal him or change his circumstance; God let him know that His Grace would carry Paul through life, even with the problem. If you stay discouraged about something you want out of your life, remember, God's Grace is sufficient until, if ever, He changes the circumstance.

Day 22. Matthew 19:26
"But Jesus beheld them, and said unto them, With men this is impossible; but with God all things are possible."

Thought of the day: Man can only do so much. Doctors can only do so much. Our money can only do so much. But when all these areas fail, God can still do what is needed no matter how impossible it may seem.

Day 23. Ephesians 5:25
"Husbands, love your wives, even as Christ also loved the church, and gave himself for it"

Thought of the day: I don't think that most husbands love their wives as God would have them to. Some husbands might say, "If my wife would act a certain way, I would love her that much." But God loves us even when we are not worthy and that's how He wants husbands to love their wives. He doesn't mean for us to be a doormat, but He does expect us to love past their behavior as much as possible.

Day 24. Ephesians 5:22
"Wives, submit yourselves unto your own husbands, as unto the Lord."

Thought of the day: When God says for the wife to submit, He doesn't mean if it is to do something that is against God or His laws. The husband should be treating her in a way, making it her desire to submit to him. And just for the record, the Word also states, that both husband and wives should submit to each other. So, for you husbands demanding your wife to submit, are you doing it too?

Day 25. Ephesians 6:1-2
"Children, obey your parents in the Lord: for this is right. Honour thy father and mother; which is the first commandment with promise."

Thought of the day: God made a special promise to children. He said He would give long life. Maybe not in long years, but a good full life. He only wants them to obey and honor, so they can learn the valuable lessons needed in life and practice being obedient to Him later in life.

Day 26. John 15:4
"Abide in me, and I in you. As the branch cannot bear fruit of itself, except it abide in the vine; no more can ye, except ye abide in me."

Thought of the day: We abide in Christ when we read His Word, pray, and do His bidding. We begin to fall away when we allow any of these to slip out of our lives. We begin to die in our spirit if we are not daily feasting on His Word. If we continue, we will have no power over the enemy. Keep abiding in Him, for that is where your strength will lie.

Day 27. Matthew 6:19-20
"Lay not up for yourselves treasures upon earth, where moth and rust doth corrupt, and where thieves break through and steal: But lay up for yourselves treasures in heaven, where neither moth nor rust doth corrupt, and where thieves do not break through nor steal:"

Thought of the day: God is not against us having a nice home or a car and such. We should, however, be more concerned with what are we storing up in Heaven. Only what we do for Him will last. That is the only thing we will be taking with us when this life is over. How does your Heavenly bank account look?

Day 28. Ephesians 3:20-21
"Now unto him that is able to do exceeding abundantly above all that we ask or think, according to the power that worketh in us, Unto him be glory in the church by Christ Jesus throughout all ages, world without end. Amen."

Thought of the day: God can and does more for us than we can even dream of. He is our total provider. Without Him, we are nothing and can do nothing. There is nothing too big for God. Just give Him a try. What mountain are you facing, God can make a way where there is no way.

Day 29. 2 Chronicles 7:14
"If my people, which are called by my name, shall humble themselves, and pray, and seek my face, and turn from their wicked ways; then will I hear from heaven, and will forgive their sin, and will heal their land."

Thought of the day: I often hear people debate on who to vote for. Who will help our country be a better place? Although man certainly has a part in how our country fairs, the biggest weight is on how God's people (not the world or politics) are doing. Are they living Holy or in the world? If they are in the world, God cannot and will not bless us. If you want change in America and you are a Christian, you can help bring that change. Live your life pleasing before God and pray for revival for you and our country.

Day 30. Ephesians 6:12
"For we wrestle not against flesh and blood, but against principalities, against powers, against the rulers of the darkness of this world, against spiritual wickedness in high places."

Thought of the day: Our fights and troubles are not always from our friends, loved ones, or human enemies. Satan may use these things to bring about trouble in our lives, but almost all of it comes as a direct attack by Satan. Yes, men do his bidding, but he is the orchestrator of the chaos. Let's try to remember that, the next time we are attacked by a friend or a loved one. Remember also, that God uses man as well to bring His bidding. Are you doing a good job of bringing the Good News to others?

Overcoming Words for July

Chapter 8

Day 1. Isaiah 14:13-15
"For thou hast said in thine heart, I will ascend into heaven, I will exalt my throne above the stars of God: I will sit also upon the mount of the congregation, in the sides of the north: I will ascend above the heights of the clouds; I will be like the most High. Yet thou shalt be brought down to hell, to the sides of the pit."

Thought of the day: We should never boast in what we can or cannot do. We should always say, "If it is the Lord's Will," we will do such and such. God hates for something to try to exalt itself above Him. To do that is almost like trying to be a god above Him. He will not share His authority or position. Allow God to be God and you just His servant, by allowing your life to flow in the direction He wants it to go.

Day 2. 1 John 4:11
"Beloved, if God so loved us, we ought also to love one another."

Thought of the day: God wants us to love one another so much, that He has put it in His Word many times to do so. If God says something once, it is final, but if He says something more than once, you might want to obey what it is He is saying. He must feel it is important to repeat Himself.

Day 3. Matthew 5:10
"Blessed are they which are persecuted for righteousness' sake: for theirs is the kingdom of heaven."

Thought of the day: God will never be outgiven. When we are persecuted for our Faith, God will always reward us with something so great, that it will make it worthwhile to go through whatever we are going through.

Day 4. Mark 11:26
"But if ye do not forgive, neither will your Father which is in heaven forgive your trespasses."

Thought of the day: Christ gave an example of this in a story of a man who owed a debt and was forgiven. But then the man who had been forgiven had another man that owed him much less and yet this guy; didn't forgive the lesser debtor, but rather had him punished. All of us deserved death, but God's love forgave our debt. It should be our privilege and honor to return that favor to others who may need to be forgiven by us. I don't want God to stop forgiving me because of my not willing to forgive others. Do you?

Day 5. Romans 8:14
"For as many as are led by the Spirit of God, they are the sons of God."

Thought of the day: When we accept Jesus Christ, we automatically are adopted as children of God. However, we still should be obedient children and not bring shame to His name. To do this, we must walk in the Spirit of God. The Holy Spirit gently guides and convicts us so we can be pleasing to the Lord. Let the Holy Spirit lead you in your journey of life.

Day 6. Psalm 103:12
"As far as the east is from the west, so far hath he removed our transgressions from us."

Thought of the day: I love this example. If you were to start at any point on the equator, you could go around the world in that direction, say west, and never reach the east. The reason being is, no matter where you stop, you are in the center of east and west. If the earth were flat, it would still be the same; you would never be able to reach the east from the west. We often keep our guilts of failures, but if we have asked God to forgive us and repented, He doesn't remember it, so why should we? Get up, dust yourself off, and start again afresh.

Day 7. Matthew 7:20
"Wherefore by their fruits ye shall know them".

Thought of the day: Most people make good fruit inspectors. They look at others and judge other people by their actions. But how often have you inspected your own fruit? Is it producing the right kind? If not, get grafted back into Christ's vine and produce good fruit, so that when others judge your fruit, they will know it came from the Master's field.

Day 8. Revelation 21:4
"And God shall wipe away all tears from their eyes; and there shall be no more death, neither sorrow, nor crying, neither shall there be any more pain: for the former things are passed away."

Thought of the day: Wouldn't it be terrible to get to Heaven to only find out that we can still have heartache? Maybe a loved one didn't make it to Heaven, and we are crying for them. Heaven, would never be Heaven, if we had to live with that for eternity. But our Gracious God will wipe away the tears and bad memories so that we can enjoy all He has for us forever. He has left no stone unturned in His plan for us.

Day 9. Psalm 107:20
"He sent his word, and healed them, and delivered them from their destructions."

Thought of the day: Praise and worship are not only good but needed in serving God. But if praise and worship take the place over the preaching of God's Word, we do people an injustice. It is ONLY through the Word of God, that will bring men to Salvation and healing. We need the Word daily. It is His Word that will bring lasting change.

Day 10. Luke 12:32
"Fear not, little flock; for it is your Father's good pleasure to give you the kingdom."

Thought of the day: As with an earthly father. God wants to bless His children with good gifts. He is willing to give us the whole kingdom if we will be obedient children. God has it all to give; He owns it all. Bask in the goodness of God and don't worry. He will take good care of you.

Day 11. 1 Corinthians 15:55
"O death, where is thy sting? O grave, where is thy victory?"

Thought of the day: The reason death has no sting over the believer; is because we won't face death. We pass from this life to the next. Only those that never accept Christ will taste death. They pass from spiritual and physical death here, to spiritual and physical death on the other side. God will give you the Grace to pass over when your time comes to leave this world if you are one of His.

Day 12. James 1:19
"Wherefore, my beloved brethren, let every man be swift to hear, slow to speak, slow to wrath:"

Thought of the day: If we would only listen more and speak less, we would get ourselves in so much less trouble. When we don't listen well, we mistake things we hear or take it out of context. This leaves us angry and upset, which sometimes leads to a negative action. Listen carefully. Ask questions to make sure what you think you heard is indeed a fact. There is a reason God gave us two ears and one mouth.

Day 13. Galatians 3:28
"There is neither Jew nor Greek, there is neither bond nor free, there is neither male nor female: for ye are all one in Christ Jesus."

Thought of the day: Christ could never be considered a racist or bigot. He loves us all. To Him, we are His workmanship. We have no identity as far as partiality, more than that. He is Just in His dealings with ALL mankind. He has that same concept when it comes to saving the lost. He wants everyone, black, white, yellow, purple, male or female, rich or poor, young or old to come to Him. Have you accepted His open border invitation?

Day 14. Proverbs 4:7
"Wisdom is the principal thing; therefore, get wisdom: and with all thy getting get understanding."

Thought of the day: You can have knowledge and not have wisdom. Knowledge without wisdom can cause hurt and pain. Wisdom normally comes from the failed trials we have faced in life. We learn from those mistakes. A good example is older people. When people are young, they are willing to jump off the highest mountain without thought or fear. But the experienced older person understands, that could be a life or death situation and chooses not to do so. You don't have to learn the hard way, you can trust in the wisdom of the ages, Jesus Christ, for the answers. If you do that, you can avoid the hurt and pains of bad choices in life.

Day 15. Luke 6:45
"A good man out of the good treasure of his heart bringeth forth that which is good; and an evil man out of the evil treasure of his heart bringeth forth that which is evil: for of the abundance of the heart his mouth speaketh."

Thought of the day: If you hang around a person, you will soon find out who they really are. At first glance, they may appear like they have the world by the tail. But once you spend some time with them, whatever is in their heart, soon will surface. When that happens, you will see the real them. Only by being around them awhile, and while they are going through things, will you know what kinda person they really are.

Day 16. Matthew 24:42
"Watch therefore: for ye know not what hour your Lord doth come."

Thought of the day: I see young people all the time thinking they can have their fun and later turn to Christ. The sad thing is, the graveyard is full of young people too. Older people also think the same thing. They think that on a later day, they will serve Christ. We don't know what our last day will be, so we should be like Christ and do the Father's Will while we have the time to do so.

Day 17. Jude 1:24-25
"Now unto him that is able to keep you from falling, and to present you faultless before the presence of his glory with exceeding joy, To the only wise God our Saviour, be glory and majesty, dominion and power, both now and ever. Amen."

Thought of the day: "What can take away my sins? Nothing but the Blood of Jesus. What can make me whole again? Nothing but the Blood of Jesus." Only through the plan of God and the power of the Blood of His Son Jesus Christ, can we stand FAULTLESS before God's Glory. Give Him praise for making way for us to stand before God. The Blood has covered our faults.

Day 18. Psalm 139:12
"Yea, the darkness hideth not from thee; but the night shineth as the day: the darkness and the light are both alike to thee."

Thought of the day: Nothing is hidden from God. The Bible says that man likes darkness because his deeds are evil. The dark gives us a false sense that God can't see what we are doing, but God sees through the darkest of night just as well as in the daytime. His eye is ever watching.

Day 19. Hebrews 12:2
"Looking unto Jesus the author and finisher of our faith; who for the joy that was set before him endured the cross, despising the shame, and is set down at the right hand of the throne of God."

Thought of the day: It was Christ's pleasure, to go to the Cross for us. He willingly did it. That shows the deep love that He has for us. We look to Him and Him only to make sure we enter the Throne of God. And because of His obedience to the Father, He now sits on the Throne as King of Kings and Lord of Lords and one day will reign on earth as He does in Heaven.

Day 20. Isaiah 61:10
"I will greatly rejoice in the Lord, my soul shall be joyful in my God; for he hath clothed me with the garments of salvation, he hath covered me with the robe of righteousness, as a bridegroom decketh himself with ornaments, and as a bride adorneth herself with her jewels."

Thought of the day: If you have nothing else that God has ever done for you, you should thank Him for the rest of eternity for the simple fact of Him paying your Sin debt through accepting His Son's Blood that was shed for you. Take the time to think of where you would be without that, and where you would be heading. When you are not getting everything you want here on earth, remember what He did for you so that one day, you could have it all.

Day 21. 1 Samuel 16:7
"But the Lord said unto Samuel, Look not on his countenance, or on the height of his stature; because I have refused him: for the Lord seeth not as man seeth; for man looketh on the outward appearance, but the Lord looketh on the heart."

Thought of the day: When we look for a leader, we look on the outward appearance. We feel they should be tall, strong, smart and full of charisma. But when it comes to being a leader or warrior for God, He doesn't look at any of those. God knows that if anything is going to be done, it is going to be through Himself, not man's ability. He chooses who He wants to lead, and like David, sometimes it is the least expected. But when given a chance, the least expected through the power of God will bring down giants.

Day 22. Ephesians 3:17-19
"That Christ may dwell in your hearts by faith; that ye, being rooted and grounded in love, May be able to comprehend with all saints what is the breadth, and length, and depth, and height; And to know the love of Christ, which passeth knowledge, that ye might be filled with all the fulness of God."

Thought of the day: The only way to even begin to understand the love of God is by being saved and walking in the goodness of God. When that happens, you see the love of God in all aspects of your life, from forgiveness of your sins to caring for you on your daily walk. By being in His love, you also will begin to have His love overflow from you to others. It's more than "Jesus loves me this I know, for the Bible tells me so." It then becomes, Jesus loves me this I know because I have experienced His love personally.

Day 23. 1 John 4:18
"There is no fear in love; but perfect love casteth out fear: because fear hath torment. He that feareth is not made perfect in love."

Thought of the day: The Bible says, God has not given us the spirit of fear. Fear is an attribute of the enemy. I have seen men married to women, trying to control the woman to love him through fear. That is not love, that is fear and only fear. Love gives because a person feels safe and secure with someone. Anytime fear comes into your life; it is to try and control you. Resist the fear and trust in Christ to be victorious.

Day 24. Psalm 37:5
"Commit thy way unto the Lord; trust also in him; and he shall bring it to pass."

Thought of the day: It is only through being obedient that we can claim any promises made by God. God will not bless a person who is walking in disobedience. Oh, He might bless them for a season, waiting for them to repeat, but eventually, He will cut them off from the blessings and begin the chastisement.

Day 25. Matthew 7:24
"Therefore whosoever heareth these sayings of mine, and doeth them, I will liken him unto a wise man, which built his house upon a rock."

Thought of the day: It is not just hearing the Word of God but obeying the Word of God. People go to church Sunday after Sunday and never apply the Word they heard. This does them no good. But when they apply the Word, the Word will become alive and work in their lives. Are you applying what God has spoken to you?

Day 26. John 14:16-17
"And I will pray the Father, and he shall give you another Comforter, that he may abide with you for ever; Even the Spirit of truth; whom the world cannot receive, because it seeth him not, neither knoweth him: but ye know him; for he dwelleth with you, and shall be in you."

Thought of the day: Praise God for sending the Holy Spirit. He is part of the Godhead. He will lead you into all truth and will warn you of dangers ahead. Imagine, God Himself, living in your mortal body. This should make you try to live the best you can, knowing that whatever you do or wherever you go, God is going with you and experiencing what you are doing.

Day 27. John 14:2-3
"In my Father's house are many mansions: if it were not so, I would have told you. I go to prepare a place for you. And if I go and prepare a place for you, I will come again, and receive you unto myself; that where I am, there ye may be also."

Thought of the day: We didn't deserve our Salvation, yet God loves us so much, that He is making a beautiful, glorious place for us to dwell with Him throughout eternity. And you can rest assured that you will enter there because Christ rose from the grave as He promised; You can rest assured He will come and get you as He promised.

Day 28. Proverbs 3:5
"Trust in the Lord with all thine heart; and lean not unto thine own understanding."

Thought of the day: It is hard to trust in something you can't see. In our mind, if we can't see it, touch it, or smell it, it doesn't exist. It reminded me of a story of a blackout in New York City. A patrol officer came by a young boy beside a telephone pole all by himself. The officer asked the boy why he wasn't afraid. The boy answered that his dad was right above him. The officer looked and couldn't see anyone. The officer said, "Son, I don't see anyone up there." The boy said, "My father is on the top of that pole working on the lines, and if I yell, you will see him faster than you can imagine." That is how it is with our Heavenly Father, you might not see Him, but if you call out for help, He will be there in a flash.

Day 29. John 10:28
"And I give unto them eternal life; and they shall never perish, neither shall any man pluck them out of my hand."

Thought of the day: Your Salvation is eternal. The reason is, because it is in the power of Christ that we have it. He holds us in His hand. We are not holding onto His. Nothing is stronger than the hand of God. So, we are secured until the day of redemption.

Day 30. Romans 8:15
"For ye have not received the spirit of bondage again to fear; but ye have received the Spirit of adoption, whereby we cry, Abba, Father."

Thought of the day: Before you trusted Christ, we were slaves unto Sin. Satan was the one you served, and Satan was the one you chose to be your father. Once you have received Salvation, Christ bought you with His Blood and adopted you into His family. We now call God Father, and He calls us His children. What a privilege to be heirs and joint-heirs with Christ Jesus.

Day 31. Philippians 4:19
"But my God shall supply all your need according to his riches in glory by Christ Jesus."

Thought of the day: Notice that the Word says God will supply all your NEEDS, not your wants. Most of the time when we are praying for something, it is something that we just want. God is only concerned with taking good care of us by giving what we need. He will always supply our needs. We sometimes don't believe that because we haven't gotten things, we thought we needed. They were just things we desired to have. Trust in the fact that God will ALWAYS supply your needs.

Overcoming Words for August

Chapter 9

Day 1. Matthew 6:34
"Take therefore no thought for the morrow: for the morrow shall take thought for the things of itself. Sufficient unto the day is the evil thereof."

Thought of the day: We worry too much. God has already said He would take care of our needs. It has been said that 90% of the things we worry about never comes. Worry is actually a sin. It probably is a sin to worry, because as a child of God, it seems to say that God can't handle what you are about to face or are facing. Do you really believe that God has everything in control? It is like the example where a person has another person blindfolded and told to fall backward to allow the other to catch them. It is hard for us to do that because we are afraid they will drop us. But God is strong enough that you can completely trust that He has you covered. Trust Him and watch Him work on your behalf.

Day 2. Acts 4:12
"Neither is there salvation in any other: for there is none other name under heaven given among men, whereby we must be saved."

Thought of the day: Many movie stars and others have made the statement that there are many ways to God, but that simply is not true. Christ said the He is the only way to the Father. If you are going to make it to Heaven, you must trust in Christ. That is not an option. There is one God, and that is the God of Abraham, Isaac, and Jacob. All other gods must bow to Him.

Day 3. Exodus 3:14
"And God said unto Moses, I Am That I Am: and he said, Thus shalt thou say unto the children of Israel, I Am hath sent me unto you."

Thought of the day: God used the word I AM, to show that He was God all by Himself. Who is the one that can heal me in my time of need? I AM. Who is the one that I can depend on for my finances need? I AM. Who is the one that I can call when I am hurting, and in despair, I AM! No matter what it is you need in life, the one you call is the I AM. He is that I AM!!!

Day 4. Isaiah 61:1
"The Spirit of the Lord God is upon me; because the Lord hath anointed me to preach good tidings unto the meek; he hath sent me to bind up the brokenhearted, to proclaim liberty to the captives, and the opening of the prison to them that are bound;"

Thought of the day: We all have been called to spread the Good News of Christ. Proclaim it on the rooftops. Let the world know what God has to offer to a dying world!

Day 5. Psalm 51:10
"Create in me a clean heart, O God; and renew a right spirit within me."

Thought of the day: We through the constant bombardment of this world and its allurements, sometimes get our hearts dirty. The only one we can turn to is God to cleanse us up. We need to keep our hearts clean to be useful in His Kingdom.

Day 6. Acts 13:22
"And when he had removed him, he raised up unto them David to be their king; to whom also he gave their testimony, and said, I have found David the son of Jesse, a man after mine own heart, which shall fulfil all my will."

Thought of the day: Those of us who know the whole life of David, has a hard time with the statement, "a man after mine own heart, which shall fulfil all my will." We know he committed adultery. He had a man killed. He tried to cover it up. And the story goes on. But what made David a man after God's heart to me, was that he was quick to want to ask for forgiveness, and in his heart, he wanted to live right before God. Aren't you glad that even though men judge from the outward, God judges us by our heart?

Day 7. Judges 16:20
"And she said, The Philistines be upon thee, Samson. And he awoke out of his sleep, and said, I will go out as at other times before, and shake myself. And he wist not that the Lord was departed from him."

Thought of the day: Samson was playing in the enemies' camp. He had defeated all of his enemies without any trouble. What he failed to remember is that it was through the power of God that he was able to do all that. He continued to dabble in sin, resting on the belief that God would always be there to defend him and by him trusting in his own strength. But finally, he crossed the line. He didn't even know that God's protective power had left him till it was too late. Don't be foolish like Samson. You can't play in the Devils sandbox and still be a powerful soldier of the Cross.

Day 8. Genesis 6:3
"And the Lord said, My spirit shall not always strive with man, for that he also is flesh: yet his days shall be an hundred and twenty years."

Thought of the day: There is a constant battle for man's soul. The enemy is trying to get man to deny and walk away from God, while God is trying to pull him close to Him. God will not continue to deal with a person who is bent on, not coming to Him. This is true even for a saved person. God wants people who want to serve Him, not be forced to. We can push God away so much, that He will allow Satan to have his way with us, but yet keep our soul saved through His power. That is not a place a Christian wants to be in. But worse, is when He gives up on dealing with a lost person. The Holy Spirit is what draws men to Christ. Without that drawing, it is not guaranteed that the lost will ever come to Christ on his own. Best to be quick to respond when God speaks.

Day 9. Leviticus 19:31
"Regard not them that have familiar spirits, neither seek after wizards, to be defiled by them: I am the Lord your God.

Thought of the day: People want to know what is ahead in their lives. Some go to card readers; some go to the horoscope or maybe an Ouija board. Many think these things are harmless, but they are directly from Satan himself. As Christians, we should never be caught doing those things. We live by faith and trust that God is in control. That is all we need to know about our future.

Day 10. Romans 8:26-27
"Likewise the Spirit also helpeth our infirmities: for we know not what we should pray for as we ought: but the Spirit itself maketh intercession for us with groanings which cannot be uttered. And he that searcheth the hearts knoweth what is the mind of the Spirit, because he maketh intercession for the saints according to the will of God."

Thought of the day: I am so glad that God didn't answer some of the dumb prayers I prayed. You might be praying for a certain car, wife, or job, not knowing that it will cause you trouble later in life. It is during those times, and times when you hurt so bad you can't even find words to say, that the Holy Spirit interprets the true desire that you have in your life. Like with the car for instance; You want a certain one, but the Spirit says: "He needs transportation." For the wife you want, the Spirit says, "He needs companionship." God knows what we truly need and what is best for us to meet that need.

Day 11. 2 Corinthians 4:8-9
"We are troubled on every side, yet not distressed; we are perplexed, but not in despair; Persecuted, but not forsaken; cast down, but not destroyed;"

Thought of the day: Being a Christian doesn't exempt us from troubles in this life. As a matter of fact, the Bible tells us that we will have trials and tribulations. But it also lets us know that we will overcome them because Christ overcame them. It is hard sometimes, but rest assured, you will not be defeated by this world, but God will deliver you as long as you are walking and trusting in Him.

Day 12. Psalm 46:2
"Therefore will not we fear, though the earth be removed, and though the mountains be carried into the midst of the sea;"

Thought of the day: Always stand firm in the faith that God is in control. Our world seems to be falling apart, but we are not of this world. He will carry us through until we get to our final destination.

Day 13. John 1:1
"In the beginning was the Word, and the Word was with God, and the Word was God."

Thought of the day: Christ has always been around. Before the world was made, Christ was there. When man was made in the garden, Christ was there. When man fell, Christ was there. No matter what you have gone through, Christ has been there. So, when things get too hard, turn to the one that said He would never leave you or desert you. He is standing just waiting for your call.

Day 14. 1 Kings 19:11-12
"And he said, Go forth, and stand upon the mount before the Lord. And, behold, the Lord passed by, and a great and strong wind rent the mountains, and brake in pieces the rocks before the Lord; but the Lord was not in the wind: and after the wind an earthquake; but the Lord was not in the earthquake: And after the earthquake a fire; but the Lord was not in the fire: and after the fire a still small voice."

Thought of the day When many people are praying to God for an answer or to guide them in a direction, they look for a sign. They want something that will really stand out. Some even go as far as saying something like, "if you want me to go to Africa, let the preacher say, 'God is calling you' in his sermon". But normally, when God is talking to us, He just speaks in a small voice. It's like some kids. You don't get the attention of some unruly kids unless you yell. But obedient children are listening to hear from their parents. If we are walking close to God and obeying Him, all it takes is a whisper, and we can hear Him.

Day 15. Matthew 28:18
"And Jesus came and spake unto them, saying, All power is given unto me in heaven and in earth."

Thought of the day: All power was given to Christ. Even the power to hold onto life until He said He was ready to die. Death is an appointment that none of us has the power to stop. Not even doctors can stop it when it's your time to die. But Christ, not only has to power to hang onto his life but has the power to raise himself up after death. He has the power to keep you too, and one day will raise you up to life everlasting.

Day 16. Isaiah 43:2
"When thou passest through the waters, I will be with thee; and through the rivers, they shall not overflow thee: when thou walkest through the fire, thou shalt not be burned; neither shall the flame kindle upon thee."

Thought of the day: It is not to say that we will not feel the effects of things that come our way, but in the end, it will not have its power over us. Whatever comes our way, God will make a way of escape.

Day 17. Matthew 6:10
"Thy kingdom come, Thy will be done in earth, as it is in heaven."

Thought of the day: God's Will shall be done on earth, and nothing can stop that. But I want you to think of this. God created us out of the dust of the earth. He also said that the Holy Spirit will abide **in** us. Since we are made of the earth, and the Holy Spirit is within us, are we allowing God's will to be done **in** earth (us) as it is in Heaven?

Day 18. John 10:14
"I am the good shepherd, and know my sheep, and am known of mine."

Thought of the day: The only way a sheep will hear the voice of their shepherd is by staying beside him enough to know what his voice is like. I have had the privilege to go to Israel and watch as 5 or 6 shepherds would have their sheep all mixed up. When one shepherd was ready to leave, he would stand up and make a sound, then start walking. Immediately, his sheep and only his sheep would raise their heads and begin to follow. Have you been near enough to our Shepherd Jesus Christ, to know when He is calling you?

Day 19. John 3:2
"The same came to Jesus by night, and said unto him, Rabbi, we know that thou art a teacher come from God: for no man can do these miracles that thou doest, except God be with him."

Thought of the day: Nicodemus was a Pharisee and a ruler of the Jews. The Pharisees were looking for the Messiah, but they didn't believe that Jesus was him. But even Nicodemus couldn't deny the power that Christ had and the life He lived. We should live that kind of life in front of others, that even though they might not believe Christ is the Son of God, our power and life should persuade them to want to learn more.

Day 20. John 4:23
"But the hour cometh, and now is, when the true worshippers shall worship the Father in spirit and in truth: for the Father seeketh such to worship him."

Thought of the day: God is not impressed by people that want to come to Him for all He has to offer Him. He wants people that will come to Him, to give Him Glory and Praise and to be willing to do His Will. Are you following God as just a get out of jail card? That is not true worship. Worship is adoration, and God deserves that and more.

Day 21. Luke 18:41
"Saying, What wilt thou that I shall do unto thee? And he said, Lord, that I may receive my sight."

Thought of the day: This blind man could have asked Christ for money, fame, or popularity. But his biggest need was to be able to see. To be able to see would give him freedom to move about, work for himself, and be independent. We, along with lost people, need our spiritual sight more than any earthly thing. It too will give us the freedom and independence through the power of God.

Day 22. Hebrews 4:15
"For we have not an high priest which cannot be touched with the feeling of our infirmities; but was in all points tempted like as we are, yet without sin."

Thought of the day: Christ didn't have to experience every temptation that man would have, but He wanted to so that He could identify with the struggles we face. And now that He overcame all of the temptations without sinning, we have been given power over sin. We will never be sinless, but at least it doesn't have to have dominion over us anymore.

Day 23. Romans 8:17
"And if children, then heirs; heirs of God, and joint-heirs with Christ; if so be that we suffer with him, that we may be also glorified together."

Thought of the day: We as believers love to claim the promises of God, but few of us want to go through what it takes to claim those promises. Christ said for us to take up our cross and follow Him. Life is not to be a bed of roses, but if we live for Christ during those hard times, He will give us our reward and we can share in His Glory.

Day 24. John 8:32
"And ye shall know the truth, and the truth shall make you free."

Thought of the day: Truth helps us more than anything. If I have cancer, I don't want my doctor to say something just to make me feel better and tell me everything is fine. No, I need the truth, so I can get the help I need. Christ said, "I am the way, the truth, and the light." We can trust He will tell exactly what we need in our life. In that, we will find freedom.

Day 25. Matthew 5:23-24
"Therefore if thou bring thy gift to the altar, and there rememberest that thy brother hath ought against thee; Leave there thy gift before the altar, and go thy way; first be reconciled to thy brother, and then come and offer thy gift."

Thought of the day: Are you aware that 6 of the 10 commandments are how we deal with mankind? God wants us to treat people right. You can be as spiritual acting as you want, but if you have a problem with your brother in Christ, then Christ has a problem with you. He wants us to live in harmony with others. And when we don't, He just might not answer your prayers for what you need.

Day 26. John 15:5
"I am the vine, ye are the branches: He that abideth in me, and I in him, the same bringeth forth much fruit: for without me ye can do nothing."

Thought of the day: If you want to be a leader and a soul winner, you must be an obedient servant for Christ. I know this is often repeated, but it is so important, it is worth repeating. We don't have strength in ourselves; all power comes from God, and the only way to have that is by abiding in Him.

Day 27. John 18:17
"Then saith the damsel that kept the door unto Peter, Art not thou also one of this man's disciples? He saith, I am not."

Thought of the day: Would you ever dream of denying the Lord? Peter actually walked with Christ for 3 years. He witnessed Christ's power and Glory, yet he denied the Lord. That can easily happen when we are in the midst of the enemies' camp. Be careful where you find yourself and the company you are keeping. You could be getting yourself into a predicament to have to make a hard stand, and you might not have the strength to do so.

Day 28. 1 Corinthians 15:9
"For I am the least of the apostles, that am not meet to be called an apostle, because I persecuted the church of God."

Thought of the day: Paul felt so guilty of the things he did against God before his conversion, that he felt like a nobody in the work of the Lord. I believe this is part of why he worked and suffered so much after his conversion. Although Paul didn't seem to be able to forgive himself, God had already not only forgiven Paul but had forgotten what he had done. He will do the same for you if you will repent. Don't be surprised, however, when Satan brings your past back up. After all, he is the accuser of the brethren. Just remember when he does, what you did is under the Blood.

Day 29. John 20:30-31
"And many other signs truly did Jesus in the presence of his disciples, which are not written in this book: But these are written, that ye might believe that Jesus is the Christ, the Son of God; and that believing ye might have life through his name."

Thought of the day: The Bible in other places says that all the things that Christ did, that the world couldn't contain all the books for it to be written in. With just the things that have been written, however, is plenty enough for us to believe that Christ is the Son of God. Christ is the only way to God. And that Christ has all power. Trust in what has been recorded; for it is the only way to Salvation.

Day 30. Psalm 34:8
"O taste and see that the Lord is good: blessed is the man that trusteth in him."

Thought of the day: God is good. The people that say otherwise have never experienced His goodness, love, and forgiveness. The only way you can tell if something is good or not is to try it for yourself. That is what He is compelling you to do now Try and see for yourself.

Day 31. John 8:12

"Then spake Jesus again unto them, saying, I am the light of the world: he that followeth me shall not walk in darkness, but shall have the light of life."

Thought of the day: Have you ever got up to use the restroom in the middle of the night and not turn on a light? 9 times out of 10, you are going to hit your big toe!! As long as we are walking with Christ, His light will guide us through the darkest of nights and not be harmed.

Overcoming Words for September

Chapter 10

Day 1. Proverbs 9:10
"The fear of the Lord is the beginning of wisdom: and the knowledge of the holy is understanding."

Thought of the day: Many people today have no fear of God. God is not talking about a fear that makes you afraid. This is a reverence type fear like you would have with a parent. People have no problem taking His name in vain or vandalizing a church building. It is by reverent fear that a new believer begins their walk with God out of love. We also gain knowledge of the triune God which is God the Father, God the Son and God the Holy Ghost. Once we begin to learn of the power and position of God, we learn how to respect His power and live with a clear understanding that when we do wrong, there will be a price to pay.

Day 2. Acts 17:28
"For in him we live, and move, and have our being; as certain also of your own poets have said, For we are also his offspring."

Thought of the day: We can do nothing without God. Think about it for a moment. Would you remember to tell your heart to beat 60 to 70 times a minute 24/7? Would you be able to control all the other things going on in your body at the same time? Of course not. But still, many think they can do it all on their own. There is the story of a man who said he could do anything God could do. So, the challenge was to make a man out of the dirt of the earth. The man began to bend down to pick up some dirt. When the person overseeing the challenge saw that, he said, "No cheating, you have to make your own dirt". Even the air we breathe comes from God. There is nothing that is, that has not been made by Him. We need Him more than we realize.

Day 3. Matthew 1:23
"Behold, a virgin shall be with child, and shall bring forth a son, and they shall call his name Emmanuel, which being interpreted is, God with us."

Thought of the day: The greatest gift this world was ever given was the birth of our Lord and Savior. However, if you don't receive this gift, then it is no value to you. Without the gift of Christ Jesus, you will not only miss Him here in this world, but you will be eternally separated from Him in the eternity to come. I am so glad that God had a plan to send His Son to die in my stead and I accepted it.

Day 4. John 6:67-68
"Then said Jesus unto the twelve, Will ye also go away? Then Simon Peter answered him, Lord, to whom shall we go? thou hast the words of eternal life."

Thought of the day: Without Christ, there is no place to turn. Only through Him is peace, contentment, our Salvation, our joy, our hope, our provision, and healing. Where else can we find that? He is our all and all!

Day 5. Revelation 21:6
"And he said unto me, It is done. I am Alpha and Omega, the beginning and the end. I will give unto him that is athirst of the fountain of the water of life freely."

Thought of the day: Christ completed all that needed to be done on Calvary. Now that He has victory over the grave and Satan, He has all authority and power. It is because of that, when we need to be filled and renewed, He can give us what we need. Not only life, but abundant life He will give to those who come to Him.

Day 6. Amos 3:3
"Can two walk together, except they be agreed?"

Thought of the day: When two people can't get along, it becomes a toxic relationship. There will always be fussing and disagreements on what to do, where to go, how long to stay, etc. For us to live a joyful life with Christ, we are the ones that must agree with Him because He has all the truth and answers. We can trust in agreement with Him too because we know that He will only do what is best for us.

Day 7. John 14:19
"Yet a little while, and the world seeth me no more; but ye see me: because I live, ye shall live also."

Thought of the day: There were people who actually witnessed Christ, His death, and His resurrection. But Christ told Thomas, blessed is he who hasn't seen but still believes. I personally have not seen God, but I know that He exists in not only the creation that He made but also because of the life I have and the conversations I have with Him daily. Billy Graham was asked one time, "How do you know that God lives"? Billy Graham replied, "Because I talked to Him just today" If you are truly His, His witness will bear witness with you, and you will know that He is alive.

Day 8. Isaiah 6:8
"Also I heard the voice of the Lord, saying, Whom shall I send, and who will go for us? Then said I, Here am I; send me."

Thought of the day: Christ was quick and ready to be sent from God to make the sacrifice for our sins. Are you quick and ready to go when God needs your service for something? Maybe it is to give for a project at church, maybe to speak to someone about their Salvation or maybe it's to go to the mission fields. We should be like the minutemen of old, and be ready to go in a moment when He calls.

Day 9. 1 Corinthians 11:29-30
"For he that eateth and drinketh unworthily, eateth and drinketh damnation to himself, not discerning the Lord's body. For this cause many are weak and sickly among you, and many sleep."

Thought of the day: This is a serious warning to those who partake of the Lord's Supper. That is a Holy action, and we are saying that we are following Christ with all we have. When we have unconfessed sin in our lives and take of the Lord's Supper, we are asking for trouble. It is imperative that we ask God to forgive us of un-confessed sin before taking the Lord's Supper. The Bible says that if we confess our sins, He will forgive them and cleanse us. So, once we confess and take the Lord's Supper, we are then worthy because of the Blood of the Lamb.

Day 10. Matthew 25:40
"And the King shall answer and say unto them, Verily I say unto you, Inasmuch as ye have done it unto one of the least of these my brethren, ye have done it unto me."

Thought of the day: Would you love to be able to serve Christ in a one on one physical way? Maybe wash His feet or prepare Him a meal? Well, you can! If we do it for people who can't help themselves, Christ appreciates that so much, that He views it as you have done that deed to Him directly. Still, want to serve Christ one on one? Then go find a person with a need and meet that need.

Day 11. Luke 11:13
"If ye then, being evil, know how to give good gifts unto your children: how much more shall your heavenly Father give the Holy Spirit to them that ask him?"

Thought of the day: I was blessed to have parents that would give me good gifts during Christmas and my birthday. They were not rich, but they did the best they could do with giving me things I needed and at times wanted. Man can only give so much, but God owns it all, and more importantly, He will never give us a gift that will harm us. He is a good Father, and because of that, you will never lack anything.

Day 12. Proverbs 6:16-19
"These six things doth the Lord hate: yea, seven are an abomination unto him: A proud look, a lying tongue, and hands that shed innocent blood, An heart that deviseth wicked imaginations, feet that be swift in running to mischief,
A false witness that speaketh lies, and he that soweth discord among brethren."

Thought of the day: Christians often love to point out that things, like homosexuality, are an abomination before God. I guess it gives them a sense of superiority because they are not guilty of it. But to God, sin is sin, and there are more things than the things we feel are more wicked, that God calls an abomination. Have you ever told a lie? Have you ever said something about someone because you heard it from another person but didn't know what they said was true? Have you ever tried to stir up things in your marriage? Have you ever felt that you were better than someone else? God said He hates those things I just mentioned. We have no right to judge another. We need to focus on keeping ourselves pure before Him more than worrying about someone else's problems. Cast the beam out of your own eye before casting the speck out of your brother's eye.

Day 13. Romans 14:12
"So then every one of us shall give account of himself to God."

Thought of the day: When you stand before God in judgment, there will be no need to try to pass the blame of your sins on someone else. You can try to blame the way you acted on your upbringing, or because of a loved one or friend, but each of us will be responsible for our own decisions to sin. It is called personal responsibility which is something our nation seems to be forgetting.

Day 14. Isaiah 40:31
"But they that wait upon the Lord shall renew their strength; they shall mount up with wings as eagles; they shall run, and not be weary; and they shall walk, and not faint."

Thought of the day: When we learn to wait on God, we will not have so much stress and worry. We will learn that in His good timing, He will answer and meet our needs. This will remove a lot of the burden others carry trying to do everything on their own. We often make our biggest mistakes in life when we rush into things. Let God answer in His perfect timing. He will be right on time, every time.

Day 15. Matthew 18:3
"And said, Verily I say unto you, Except ye be converted, and become as little children, ye shall not enter into the kingdom of heaven."

Thought of the day: Why must we become as little children when coming to Christ? Well, one reason is that a child can't take care of himself. They are dependent on an adult to give them what they need. Another thing is, they trust the parent with their future without question. They have a pure, blind trust. That is the way we must come to Christ. Knowing we can't make it on our own. Knowing that we can trust Him with everything in our lives.

Day 16. James 4:17
"Therefore to him that knoweth to do good, and doeth it not, to him it is sin."

Thought of the day: Did you know that sin doesn't always have to be something you have done? Sometimes it is when you know you should do something but refuse. Maybe it was to give a dollar to the man that was begging on the street. Maybe it was to call up someone and ask for forgiveness for the way you acted toward them. Anytime, no matter if it was an action or something you failed to do that you knew you should; it is a sin. Always try to be sensitive to the Holy Spirit and His leadership, so you make and do the right decisions.

Day 17. Deuteronomy 20:4
"For the Lord your God is he that goeth with you, to fight for you against your enemies, to save you."

Thought of the day: When we face life's battles, it is good to know that we never will face it alone. Furthermore, it is good to know that the one who is with us will fight, and win the battle that we are in.

Day 18. Matthew 5:4
"Blessed are they that mourn: for they shall be comforted."

Thought of the day: It is hard to know what to say or do when we see someone in mourning. But God knows what that person needs. When we see someone mourning, say a quick prayer for them that God will give them the comfort that only He can give. That would be the best thing we could do for them.

Day 19. Matthew 6:33
"But seek ye first the kingdom of God, and his righteousness; and all these things shall be added unto you."

Thought of the day: We normally have this backward. We spend most of our time trying to work and obtain things. It would be much easier, however, if we would focus on the Lord's work first because He has promised to take care of our needs if we will tend to Him first.

Day 20. Psalm 103:1
"Bless the Lord, O my soul: and all that is within me, bless his holy name."

Thought of the day: Because of all that God does for us, He deserves our praise. Not just a quick thank you, but a heart that is continually thankful within. He is worthy of all our praise.

Day 21. Luke 17:3-4
"Take heed to yourselves: If thy brother trespass against thee, rebuke him; and if he repent, forgive him. And if he trespass against thee seven times in a day, and seven times in a day turn again to thee, saying, I repent; thou shalt forgive him."

Thought of the day: How many times have you messed up when it comes to serving God? Once? Twice? A billion? Truth is, we mess up most of the day, even when we don't realize we are doing it. But has God ever told you that He wasn't going to forgive you? Absolutely not. We should have that same spirit with those that need our forgiveness. Mercy has been abundantly given to us; we should abundantly give Mercy to others.

Day 22. 1 Corinthians 13:4-8
"Charity suffereth long, and is kind; charity envieth not; charity vaunteth not itself, is not puffed up, Doth not behave itself unseemly, seeketh not her own, is not easily provoked, thinketh no evil; Rejoiceth not in iniquity, but rejoiceth in the truth; Beareth all things, believeth all things, hopeth all things, endureth all things. Charity never faileth: but whether there be prophecies, they shall fail; whether there be tongues, they shall cease; whether there be knowledge, it shall vanish away."

Thought of the day: The word charity here can be replaced with the word love. Want to know if someone truly loves you, go over these verses, and compare them to what the person is doing to you. Want to know if you truly love someone else? Go over these verses and see how your love compares to them. Do the same with the love you claim to have with God. Love is an action, not just a word.

Day 23. Colossians 3:5
"Mortify therefore your members which are upon the earth; fornication, uncleanness, inordinate affection, evil concupiscence, and covetousness, which is idolatry:"

Thought of the day: In today's society, we constantly have to fight the temptations to these sins mentioned above. It seems that every commercial or movie has something that appeals to the flesh. The Bible says that if we walk in the Spirit, we will not fulfill the lust of the flesh. Christ didn't ask us to give up our physical body to a physical death, but He did ask us to sacrifice our fleshly desires to serve Him and be a living sacrifice. How are you doing in that area?

Day 24. 1 John 4:8
"He that loveth not knoweth not God; for God is love."

Thought of the day: The Bible says, "Whoever claims to love God, yet hates a brother or sister is a liar." That is a very powerful statement! It is not a suggestion once again that we love one another. It is a commandment and one that God takes seriously. Ask God to give you the strength to love your enemies so that you can be pleasing to God.

Day 25. Proverbs 1:8-9
"My son, hear the instruction of thy father, and forsake not the law of thy mother: For they shall be an ornament of grace unto thy head, and chains about thy neck."

Thought of the day: Kids and young adults think their parents are old-fashioned and dumb. But the truth is, they walked down this life's journey a long time and have learned some of the pits you can fall into. It is best to learn from someone who has traveled down a path, then to stumble around on your own trying to find the way. Young people, you might just learn a thing or two if you will just let down your pride and arrogance and listen.

Day 26. John 13:34-35
A new commandment I give unto you, that ye love one another; as I have loved you, that ye also love one another. By this shall all men know that ye are my disciples, if ye have love one to another.

Thought of the day: The outward proof that you are a child of God is simple. You will have love for one another. That is in contradiction to the views of the world. The world only loves those that can help them achieve something, but the believer loves even his enemy. Can people see the love of God in your life?

Day 27. Psalm 119:9
"Wherewithal shall a young man cleanse his way? by taking heed thereto according to thy word."

Thought of the day: Obey everything you can in the Word of God and your life will be pleasing to Him. Be a doer of the Word and be quick to respond to the Holy Spirit's guidance.

Day 28. Luke 6:34
"And if ye lend to them of whom ye hope to receive, what thank have ye? for sinners also lend to sinners, to receive as much again."

Thought of the day: Have you ever given someone some money and then they give it to someone else? Did that make you angry? It shouldn't. I know our flesh wants to fuss them out, but in reality, once you have given something, it then becomes that person's property to do as they please. If you decide to give something away, don't expect a certain reaction and you won't be disappointed. Also, as this verse mainly is talking about, we shouldn't be biased as to who we do good deeds for. Friends or strangers should be the same to us when we do good for others.

Day 29. Ephesians 4:29
"Let no corrupt communication proceed out of your mouth, but that which is good to the use of edifying, that it may minister grace unto the hearers."

Thought of the day: Corrupt communication is not only cursing. Corrupt communication can be negativity, gossip, hate, and so much more. The more we allow the Holy Spirit to fill us, the less corruption will come out of us.

Day 30. Romans 10:17
"So then faith cometh by hearing, and hearing by the word of God".

Thought of the day: If we want to see someone get born again, or if there is something, we struggle with trusting God is going to take care of it; it will all change if we listen to the Word of God. The Word of God will give clear direction, confidence, conviction, or anything else we need at the moment. Read the Word every day so you can have the power and Faith to overcome anything.

Overcoming Words for October

Chapter 11

Day 1. Psalm 118:24
"This is the day which the Lord hath made; we will rejoice and be glad in it."

Thought of the day: There are good days and bad, but we should be glad in all the days we live because we have been redeemed by the Blood of the Lamb. Also, because we know that God is allowing things to happen to us to teach us something or to show His Glorious power. If you are having a bad day, go ahead and rejoice. God is still in control.

Day 2. James 2:19
"Thou believest that there is one God; thou doest well: the devils also believe, and tremble."

Thought of the day: It brings fear to me when I hear people curse or make fun of God. And especially when I hear people say there is no God. God is very patient and long-suffering and full of Mercy. You can deny God all you want, but He still exists. Even the devil and his demons are smart enough to know that. They also recognize His power as they tremble in just hearing His name.

Day 3. Deuteronomy 8:18
"But thou shalt remember the Lord thy God: for it is he that giveth thee power to get wealth, that he may establish his covenant which he sware unto thy fathers, as it is this day."

Thought of the day: It is God who allows us to gain wealth. We wouldn't have the strength or the knowledge to do anything without Christ. But even if He doesn't allow us to obtain wealth, we can rest assured that He will always supply all your needs.

Day 4. Haggai 1:6
"Ye have sown much, and bring in little; ye eat, but ye have not enough; ye drink, but ye are not filled with drink; ye clothe you, but there is none warm; and he that earneth wages earneth wages to put it into a bag with holes."

Thought of the day: When we walk outside of God's Will or especially rob Him of His tithes and offerings, we will find that no matter how much we make or indulge in life, we will find it empty and vain in the end. Life is only complete in Christ.

Day 5. Proverbs 22:1
"A good name is rather to be chosen than great riches, and loving favour rather than silver and gold."

Thought of the day: Dad always told me in school, you don't have to be smart, to be honest and good in school. He also said, watch how you live your life, because it is a reflection of our family's name. The same is true when we are children of God. We should be careful how we act; we bear His name.

Day 6. Luke 16:23
"And in hell he lift up his eyes, being in torments, and seeth Abraham afar off, and Lazarus in his bosom."

Thought of the day: To me, this is one of the saddest verses in the Bible. Can you imagine how it must feel to be fine one minute, only to find in the next, that you are burning in Hell for eternity? Don't let that happen to you. Make sure of your Salvation before it is too late.

Day 7. Revelation 22:17
"And the Spirit and the bride say, Come. And let him that heareth say, Come. And let him that is athirst come. And whosoever will, let him take the water of life freely."

Thought of the day: The wonderful thing about God's Mercy and Grace is that you don't have to be rich, of great importance or educated. He will take anyone who wants Him as their Savior. He is calling for you to surrender to Him. What are you going to do?

Day 8. Deuteronomy 30:19
"I call heaven and earth to record this day against you, that I have set before you life and death, blessing and cursing: therefore choose life, that both thou and thy seed may live:"

Thought of the day: Each day, you face decisions. You face decisions to do right or wrong. When we do wrong, and we are a child of God, we cut off fellowship with God and His blessings. That is a bad place to be but what is even worse, is when you choose not to accept God as your redemption. That is truly death in both this life and the life to come.

Day 9. 1 Corinthians 13:12
"For now we see through a glass, darkly; but then face to face: now I know in part; but then shall I know even as also I am known."

Thought of the day: We all have our ideas on what to believe about certain scriptures, but none of us can say we have all the right answers. Some things are the way we interpret it and how it means to us. But there are scriptures that we can bank on. One of them is there is no other way to get to God, but by His Son's Blood, He shed for our sins. Another is that He will never leave us and still another, that He will supply all our needs. On the things that don't really matter one way or another in the way we may view something, it is not worth fighting for. But for things that are written in stone, we should never compromise on that.

Day 10. Matthew 6:6
"But thou, when thou prayest, enter into thy closet, and when thou hast shut thy door, pray to thy Father which is in secret; and thy Father which seeth in secret shall reward thee openly."

Thought of the day: This doesn't mean that we literally go into a closet. It means to shut out all of the Worlds thoughts and stress and focus on our prayer to God. We don't have to yell out our prayer. Just a silent prayer is enough, and God will answer.

Day 11. 1 Timothy 2:5
"For there is one God, and one mediator between God and men, the man Christ Jesus;"

Thought of the day: We don't go through Budda or any other false God. It doesn't matter even if an angel tells us we can. They only one that matters is God almighty, and we should thank God for Christ being our mediator for what we do wrong. Also, we need to be glad for the fact of the Holy Spirit living in us and guiding us in the right direction.

Day 12. Matthew 6:13
"And lead us not into temptation, but deliver us from evil: For thine is the kingdom, and the power, and the glory, for ever. Amen."

Thought of the day: I saw something online the other day that seems like the truth to me. It said, "Lead me not into temptation. I can find it all by myself". It is true that temptation seems to follow us every day. It is hard to resist at times. It is a good policy to ask God to help us stay clear from those temptations. But if we still face it, it's also important to be filled with His Spirit and the Word of God to fight against it.

Day 13. Hebrews 13:4
"Marriage is honourable in all, and the bed undefiled: but whoremongers and adulterers God will judge"

Thought of the day: God designed a man and woman to want to have an intimate relationship. But He designed it to only be between a husband and wife. Once you have an intimate relationship, the Bible says they two become one flesh. When you have multiple relationships, your thoughts and feelings will waver because souls have blended. Stay pure until you get married to the one that God sends to you, so you can love each other fully and be happy, satisfying each other in the intimacy God created you to desire.

Day 14. Philippians 4:11
"Not that I speak in respect of want: for I have learned, in whatsoever state I am, therewith to be content."

Thought of the day: God never said he would bless us with a great mansion or loads of food or even a high position. He did promise to take care of all of our needs. We are spoiled in America. We feel if we don't have the nicest home, best car and lots of money, then we are missing something. But if we look at other countries and what they have, we would soon learn that we are blessed beyond measure. No matter what you have in life, be content until God brings you to a different level.

Day 15. Genesis 2:24
"Therefore shall a man leave his father and his mother, and shall cleave unto his wife: and they shall be one flesh."

Thought of the day: Many marriages have problems because the man's mother is always trying to get in the middle of the marriage. There can only be one woman in the home, and that's the wife. It is important for the husband to make his mother fully understand, that she is no longer the mouthpiece of his home, but his wife is, as the husband and wife share their lives and decisions. Husbands don't let your mother try and control your home. You and your wife are one now. There is no more room for another woman, not even your mother in your home decisions.

Day 16. Matthew 19:24
"And again I say unto you, It is easier for a camel to go through the eye of a needle, than for a rich man to enter into the kingdom of God. "

Thought of the day: The eye of a needle is not the needle we sew with. It is a small gate around the walls of Jerusalem. When camels went through, the camel driver had to remove everything that was on the camel's back, then place the camel on his knees and guide him along to get under the opening. Then, once on the other side, he had to again, load the camel. It is not impossible for a rich person to go to Heaven, but more often than not, once a person is rich, they feel they no longer need God. This is where it gets hard for them to enter in. They don't want anyone telling them how to live their lives and feel they can do it all on their own. What we all need to remember, is that none of us can do anything without God and it is only through Him that we will make it to Heaven. You can't buy your way in.

Day 17. 3 John 1:2
"Beloved, I wish above all things that thou mayest prosper and be in health, even as thy soul prospereth."

Thought of the day: God is not against money and wealth. As a matter of fact, He would love for us to have it. But He only wants us to have it if it will not come in between you and serving Him. He is more concerned with us growing in Him than blessing us with so much that we can't contain it.

Day 18. Matthew 6:7
"But when ye pray, use not vain repetitions, as the heathen do: for they think that they shall be heard for their much speaking."

Thought of the day: You don't have to learn to pray a formal prayer. God is not concerned with these and thou. He just wants the fellowship with Him. I myself sometimes just call Him dad. He said He would be our Father. He wants that intimacy with Him, not ridged and shallow. Be respectful, but talk to Him as you would any other and remember to give Him thanks for what He does and is going to do. He also doesn't want you to try and get the glory out of praying out loud around other people. He wants prayers from your heart.

Day 19. 2 Corinthians 6:14
"Be ye not unequally yoked together with unbelievers: for what fellowship hath righteousness with unrighteousness? and what communion hath light with darkness?"

Thought of the day: I have seen relationships like oil and water. No matter what kind of relationship you are in, if there are only tension and fighting and you can't get it resolved, you are in a toxic environment. Also, talk to a person for a while until you know what and how they believe. You don't want to be stuck in something that is only going to bring stress every time you are around that individual.

Day 20. Matthew 5:27-28
"Ye have heard that it was said by them of old time, Thou shalt not commit adultery: But I say unto you, That whosoever looketh on a woman to lust after her hath committed adultery with her already in his heart."

Thought of the day: Sin is not only the action we take. Sin starts in the heart and mind. It then will lead to the action. That is why God judges the heart. That is where the real you is found. If the heart is evil, it will show up in life.

Day 21. 1 Peter 2:24
"Who his own self bare our sins in his own body on the tree, that we, being dead to sins, should live unto righteousness: by whose stripes ye were healed."

Thought of the day: Everything that Christ suffered on the Cross was for a reason. He not only died for our sins but for our infirmities as well. His Blood is all-powerful. It can cleanse, heal and deliver.

Day 22. Luke 15:7
"I say unto you, that likewise joy shall be in heaven over one sinner that repenteth, more than over ninety and nine just persons, which need no repentance."

Thought of the day: Did you know that on the day that you accepted the Lord Jesus Christ as your Savior, that Heaven burst out with praise? It is kind of like when a child is born into a home, and all the relatives are around. When the doctor comes in and announces that the child has arrived, people begin to cheer, cry, hug and rejoice. It is a time of celebration. It is the same way when we are born again, and the news reaches Heaven. Everyone there is excited. You didn't know you made such an impact in Heaven, did you?

Day 23. Proverbs 6:28
"Can one go upon hot coals, and his feet not be burned?"

Thought of the day: This verse is pertaining to falling into temptation with a woman, but it fits in other applications as well. Many people, especially young people, want to just dabble a little in sin. They want to look cool and fit in. But trust me, if you play with fire, you will get burnt. It won't be long until you are surrounded by the flames and want to get out, but you won't be able to without seeing some scars of the flames when you escape.

Day 24. Ephesians 6:4
"And, ye fathers, provoke not your children to wrath: but bring them up in the nurture and admonition of the Lord."

Thought of the day: Discipline is a delicate thing. Children can get on our nerves, and sometimes we might discipline in anger. Some go as far as beating their child or saying bad things to them as they will never amount to anything and stuff like that. We need to be careful when disciplining them that we are doing it in love. If we don't do it in love, they will feel the hatred and most likely resist what we are trying to teach them. They might even develop a hatred toward the parent. Remember, God chastises us in love, and that is how we need to discipline our children.

Day 25. Luke 5:32
"I came not to call the righteous, but sinners to repentance."

Thought of the day: People who "think" they are living right, normally don't see the need to give their lives to Christ. They are filled with pride and arrogance. But someone who has never lived a good life normally doesn't feel worthy to come to Christ. But little do they know, that is the very reason He came to earth to give His life. He knew, without Him, they would die and go to Hell and be forever separated from God. It is the vilest of sinners to the lest of sinners that Christ is calling to come to Him. If you feel you are not worthy, it is you He is looking for.

Day 26. Proverbs 29:15
"The rod and reproof give wisdom: but a child left to himself bringeth his mother to shame."

Thought of the day: The problem with most young people today is both parents are normally working full-time jobs, and when they are off, they are trying to get the things around the house done. Too often kids are left to themselves. They spend hours on their cell phones and video games. Unfortunately, many of those things have evil temptations all around. Without proper training and time showing them love, before long, they most likely will get into some type of trouble. If you have kids, that was a choice you made. Now do what you should and take the time to be with them and train them.

Day 27. 1 Samuel 3:10
"And the Lord came, and stood, and called as at other times, Samuel, Samuel. Then Samuel answered, Speak; for thy servant heareth."

Thought of the day: It never ceases to amaze me, that such an awesome and powerful God will call upon a lowly human to do His bidding. God spoke the world, and all there is in existence, yet He chose to speak to man to do His Will and spread His message. What an honor for a person to be selected to do or say what the King of Kings and Lord of Lords wants to be done or said. Are you listening for His voice of instruction to you?

Day 28. Proverbs 13:22
"A good man leaveth an inheritance to his children's children: and the wealth of the sinner is laid up for the just."

Thought of the day: Our job as parents is not over once they have left home. We still need to be making sure that we have something for our kids when we leave this world. They, of course, need to be trained on how to use that money should that time come. But more than money, we need to make sure that we have left them the inheritance of a good Christian Faith and belief in Jesus Christ. If we have left that, even though we might not have had money to leave them, that Godly inheritance will carry them through the rest of their lives.

Day 29. 1 John 2:15
"Love not the world, neither the things that are in the world. If any man love the world, the love of the Father is not in him."

Thought of the day: Our main desire, if we are truly born again, is to please the Lord. When we begin to desire more of this world, it is because we have lost focus on what is important. This world and all that is in it, will one day be gone. It is normally pride that causes us to desire more and more. Pride in itself is a sin. Let's do like Paul and press toward the mark of the High Calling. It is in that; we will be successful.

Day 30. Luke 17:2
"It were better for him that a millstone were hanged about his neck, and he cast into the sea, than that he should offend one of these little ones."

Thought of the day: We need to be careful about what we do or say around other people. People, especially lost people, are watching you during all the phases of your life, good and bad times. They want to see if what you have and claim that it works, really does. If they see you stressing, cursing or doing evil, then they think to themselves, there is nothing in what you have and might not ever trust Christ. This verse might be mainly talking about how we live in front of new believers, and the same thing applies, but we need to be careful around all people, that we are letting our light shine always for Christ.

Day 31. Matthew 7:3
"And why beholdest thou the mote that is in thy brother's eye, but considerest not the beam that is in thine own eye?"

Thought of the day: It is so easy to judge others. When we are going about life, we hardly ever take out the time to see how we act or think about what we are saying and how it sounds. We most of the time, think we are doing everything right. But just like we can see the faults in everyone else, they can see the faults in us too. Take some time out each day and ask God to reveal to you where you need improving. You might just find yourself so busy trying to straighten yourself out, that you won't have time to correct others.

Overcoming Words for November

Chapter 12

Day 1. 1 Corinthians 15:19
If in this life only we have hope in Christ, we are of all men most miserable.

Thought of the day: Have you noticed in your life, that you dream of having a nice car or home; then after you get it, it soon loses its joy? The things life has to offer can never satisfy our souls. It will for a moment or two, then fade. But the life we have in Christ will always be fulfilling if we are abiding in Him.

Day 2. 1 Peter 4:8
"And above all things have fervent charity among yourselves: for charity shall cover the multitude of sins."

Thought of the day: If you see a person gossiping about another, you can rest assured that the person doesn't love the other. Most people can't wait to spread some juicy news they hear about someone. But, if you really love someone, you don't want people to view them negatively, you want to cover them. Christ loves us so much that He has covered us with His robe of righteousness so that the world won't see our sinful nakedness. That's true love!

Day 3. Ephesians 4:26-27
"Be ye angry, and sin not: let not the sun go down upon your wrath: Neither give place to the devil."

Thought of the day: God never said we can't be angry. There are things we should be angry about. We should be angry that Satan is destroying our youth. We should be angry that our nation is turning against God. But we need to be careful that we don't allow that angry to cause us to hate or act out in a destructive way or a way that will bring hurt to others. Also, make sure that what you are angry about, isn't something you caused.

Day 4. Romans 6:14
"For sin shall not have dominion over you: for ye are not under the law, but under grace."

Thought of the day: The Bible tells us that sin will not have dominion over you. That is not to say that you won't sin; you will not be a slave to it anymore. When you are saved, and you go back to the world, it doesn't give the pleasure it once gave. It leaves you feeling empty. The Grace God gives, keeps us from falling back into the slavery of sin. Thank God for His marvelous Grace that is able to keep us until we see Him face to face.

Day 5. 1 John 1:8-10
"If we say that we have no sin, we deceive ourselves, and the truth is not in us. If we confess our sins, he is faithful and just to forgive us our sins, and to cleanse us from all unrighteousness. If we say that we have not sinned, we make him a liar, and his word is not in us."

Thought of the day: I listened to a radio broadcast many years ago, and the main theme was, "we are the perfect church because we are perfect." They really believed that in their own power, they were perfect. No one is perfect on their own, even after accepting Christ. It is only through the Blood that you are righteous before God. To say otherwise, diminishes the work Christ did. We ALL have sinned and come short of the Glory of God. ALL means ALL and yes, that means you too.

Day 6. Romans 11:6
"And if by grace, then is it no more of works: otherwise grace is no more grace. But if it be of works, then it is no more grace: otherwise work is no more work. "

Thought of the day: Thank God we are saved only by Grace. We would never be able to live a life pleasing enough to make it to Heaven. It is all in the finished work of Jesus Christ as the Word says, "lest we boast."

Day 7. Exodus 20:3
"Thou shalt have no other gods before me."

Thought of the day: You might feel confident that you don't have any gods before God. But is that really true? Do you have a car that you care more about than the things of God? Maybe it is your wife and kids. Maybe it is your money or something you are passionate about. If ANYTHING is in your life that keeps you from doing what God wants you to do and being the best at it, then it is your god. Check your closet closely to make sure you don't have any gods laying around

Day 8. Matthew 10:28
"And fear not them which kill the body, but are not able to kill the soul: but rather fear him which is able to destroy both soul and body in hell."

Thought of the day: Have you ever wondered what you would do, if, in this nation, they began to kill Christians? That is a fearful thing to think about. As a matter of fact, that is where Peter found himself one day. He was in the midst of people who were crucifying Christ and looking for Christ, disciples to kill them as well. Out of fear, Peter denied he even knew Christ. Peter lost focus on who it was that he should be fearful of. Man can only take our life; God can take our soul and cast it into Hell. Man's torment will only last a few moments. The payment of sin will last for eternity. It is normal to fear when bad things are coming your way, but try and remember, it is better to go through anything in this life than to fall into the hands of an angry God.

Day 9. Romans 6:15
"What then? shall we sin, because we are not under the law, but under grace? God forbid."

Thought of the day: Christ has freed us from the penalty of sin and from us trying to work our way for Salvation. That doesn't excuse us from not trying to live Holy for Him. Instead, because of that wonderful gift, it should make us more determined to try and live right, knowing the great price Christ had to pay for our Salvation. It is not as stated before; a get out of jail free card. We need to work as a thank you, and also so that others might hear and know what Christ has to offer. Plus, we don't want to lead the world down the wrong path with them seeing us do things we shouldn't be doing.

Day 10. John 4:29
"Come, see a man, which told me all things that ever I did: is not this the Christ?"

Thought of the day: God knows all about you. Even what you do in the dark and what you think in your mind. You would think that because He knows so much about you, that He would never want you. But that is not true. He wants to make a change in your life so you can have fellowship with Him and tell others about His goodness. By the way, it is no use to try and hide something, He will know about it.

Day 11. Romans 5:20
"Moreover the law entered, that the offence might abound. But where sin abounded, grace did much more abound:"

Thought of the day: I know of many people that think they have out sinned, God's Mercy and Grace. You can never do that. The more that sin raises its ugly head, the more Mercy and Grace steps in to conquer it. Christ came to make even the vilest sinner clean. Trust Him today.

Day 12. John 8:10-11
"When Jesus had lifted up himself, and saw none but the woman, he said unto her, Woman, where are those thine accusers? hath no man condemned thee? She said, No man, Lord. And Jesus said unto her, Neither do I condemn thee: go, and sin no more."

Thought of the day: You will find no shortage of people who are ready to put you down and tell you what an awful person you are. But God will never do that. He and He alone is perfect enough to do so, but He always comes in Mercy, Grace, long-suffering, and compassion. Isn't it wonderful, that the only one that matters, will always be ready to forgive?

Day 13. John 11:44
"And he that was dead came forth, bound hand and foot with graveclothes: and his face was bound about with a napkin. Jesus saith unto them, Loose him, and let him go."

Thought of the day: This is the perfect example of a life without Christ when Christ calls for them, and they respond. When a person is physically dead, they can do nothing or hear nothing. They are cold and lifeless. But once Jesus speaks to us in our lifeless sinful bodies, we are made alive. We can move and have our being. We are free to live a lifetime of happiness in Him.

Day 14. Luke 12:39
"And this know, that if the goodman of the house had known what hour the thief would come, he would have watched, and not have suffered his house to be broken through."

Thought of the day: Most thieves enter a home in the middle of the night. They know that most likely, everyone will be asleep and not prepared should they awaken and find them there. Satan tries to do the same thing. He tries to come when you are going through your hardest test or surprise you when you least expect it. That is why it is best to stay on top of your game. Is your Bible reading and prayer life up to date? Be watching all around you so you will be ready when he comes.

Day 15. Job 1:21
"And said, Naked came I out of my mother's womb, and naked shall I return thither: the Lord gave, and the Lord hath taken away; blessed be the name of the Lord."

Thought of the day: Life is fickle. You can be on top of the world today and rock bottom tomorrow. They only thing that will never change is Christ. We came into this life with nothing, but we don't have to leave it without anything. If we have Christ, we will have it all.

Day 16. Proverbs 25:19
"Confidence in an unfaithful man in time of trouble is like a broken tooth, and a foot out of joint."

Thought of the day: I can't think of a greater pain than a toothache. I am sure all the women are saying, "Then you have never had a baby." Well, that might be true; however, when you put your trust in man, especially one that is notorious for not doing what they promise, it hurts. It's best to never put your trust and confidence in any man, except Jesus Christ. His promises are yes and amen. He is the only one that can keep what He promises to do.

Day 17. Matthew 7:21
"Not every one that saith unto me, Lord, Lord, shall enter into the kingdom of heaven; but he that doeth the will of my Father which is in heaven."

Thought of the day: The Bible tells us that many will say to God on the day of judgment, that they did mighty works for Him. But sadly, they never accepted Christ as their redemption. No matter how much you do in life for God, if you have never accepted Christ into your life, you are the same old sinner you once were. Don't let the enemy trick you into believing you are saved by your work. It is only by the Blood of Jesus, will you be able to pass the judgment of God and enter Heaven.

Day 18. Psalm 121:1
"I will lift up mine eyes unto the hills, from whence cometh my help."

Thought of the day: When life is beating you up, that is not the time to be walking around looking at the ground. Lift your head high. Put a smile on your face. Give God thanks in advance for His deliverance of your circumstance. Our power to overcome doesn't come from this world, so stop looking down. It comes from above, so begin looking up to where the victory will come.

Day 19. Proverbs 26:11
"As a dog returneth to his vomit, so a fool returneth to his folly."

Thought of the day: When a man tries to change his life on his own power, most of the time, he will go right back to the way he was. I see this so much, especially with a couple who, for instance, has a drunk as a partner. When the other partner can't handle the drunkenness and threatens to leave, the drunk says they will change. They do for a few days or maybe a week, but most of the time, they go right back to their drinking. It is through the transforming power of Jesus Christ and the power of the Holy Spirit that you can actually change for a lifetime. Stop trying to do things on your own and trust in His power that He gives freely.

Day 20. Psalm 46:1
"God is our refuge and strength, a very present help in trouble."

Thought of the day: When I was young, if I found myself in trouble, I would run to my dad. I knew that if I could get to him, I would be safe. But an earthly father can only save you from so much. He can't change things that already have taken place. He can't heal your body if you are dying. He can't forgive you of sins or save your soul. Now that I am older, when I am in need, I know who to run to. It is the one with all power to do all things. Jesus Christ.

Day 21. Luke 23:34
"Then said Jesus, Father, forgive them; for they know not what they do. And they parted his raiment, and cast lots."

Thought of the day: Can you forgive someone who has beaten you, spat on you, told lies on you and sentence you to death without a cause? I probably couldn't either. But that is what Jesus did for each and every one of us. You might not have put the nails in, and no, you weren't even there when it was done. But we all have the curse of Adam and are guilty of what happened to Christ, because the only way we could be pardoned, is by His crucifixion. He said of you to His Father as well, forgive (your name here), they don't know what they do.

Day 22. Philippians 2:5
"Let this mind be in you, which was also in Christ Jesus:"

Thought of the day: If you want to stay pleasing to God, you must put on the mind of Christ. To do that, you try to think about the decisions you make; are they going to be pleasing to Him. You don't think like the world which focuses on themselves and what they get. You also don't think of sinful, earthly desires, because you know that is against the Fathers Will. And another thing you will think is that you must be about the Father's business. These are just a few things that your mind will think differently if you are putting on the mind of Christ. Can you tell the difference in your thinking since Christ has come into your life?

Day 23. John 3:7
"Marvel not that I said unto thee, Ye must be born again."

Thought of the day: To be born again, means that you trust Christ and allow Him in your life. You also repeat or turn away from your sins. You agree with God that you are a sinner. As with a newborn baby; when it enters the world, everything is new. The same thing happens to a new believer. Everything is new! It should not be a shock that we MUST trust Christ to make it. In our earthly bodies, we are full of sin, and sin brings death. The only way to escape eternal death is by trusting Christ as your savior, (which makes you born again). There is no other way.

Day 24. Psalm 73:3
"For I was envious at the foolish, when I saw the prosperity of the wicked."

Thought of the day: Have you ever asked yourself why a person who might not even believe in God has so much? I have too. It seems many times that some of the wealthiest people are evil and corrupt. But we view their worth by this earth's standards. All that this earth has is temporal. In reality, if they don't have Christ in their lives and you do; you are far richer than they, or you, can ever imagine.

Day 25. John 4:4
"And he must needs go through Samaria."

Thought of the day: When Christ said this, it was a long journey, just to go and talk to one person. What is even more amazing, is the place He was going to was a place that a Jew wouldn't go. The people that lived there, to the Jews, were nothing more than dogs. They were worthless to them. Jesus, however, out of His short life to accomplish His mission; took the time to deal with this one, outcasted person. I am so glad that Christ took out the time one day and came to where I was. I too was worthless, but yet, He came and forgave me of my sins and took me in. Has He come by your house yet? When He does, let him in.

Day 26. Mark 5:15
"And they come to Jesus, and see him that was possessed with the devil, and had the legion, sitting, and clothed, and in his right mind: and they were afraid."

Thought of the day: When a person has a personal relationship with Jesus Christ, no matter how bad of a person they use to be, their life will be forever changed. They will not look the same, talk the same, or act the same. They say that couples after they have been married for years, begin to look like their mate. I'm not so sure about that, but I am sure, that when you walk with Jesus daily, you begin to look a lot like Him.

Day 27. Mark 16:15
"And he said unto them, Go ye into all the world, and preach the gospel to every creature."

Thought of the day: I believe, if you are going to go to another country to preach the Gospel, you had better know you were called to do so. However, even if you are not called to do so, you are commanded to preach the Gospel to those around you. The first place you need to start is in your own home. To preach the Gospel is not bashing a person's head in for the things they do wrong. It is telling them of the Good News of Christ and His power to save.

Day 28. Acts 8:6-8
"And the people with one accord gave heed unto those things which Philip spake, hearing and seeing the miracles which he did. For unclean spirits, crying with loud voice, came out of many that were possessed with them: and many taken with palsies, and that were lame, were healed. And there was great joy in that city."

Thought of the day: Any time that a person hears of the Gospel and responds to it. They will find great joy and a peace that passes understanding. It is so important that we share what Christ has done for us like Philip, did so that others can receive the miraculous gift of Salvation, healing, and peace.

Day 29. Luke 10:20
"Notwithstanding in this rejoice not, that the spirits are subject unto you; but rather rejoice, because your names are written in heaven."

Thought of the day: In some Denominations, they focus their attention on what kind of power they have over Spirits. Some even base whether you are filled with the Holy Spirit or not by speaking in another language or casting out demons. I personally don't believe you have to do all that to be filled with the Holy Spirit, but I do know, that those things fail deeply when compared with what we really should be thankful for and that is our Salvation. Our Salvation is the greatest miracle of all. Nothing should override that for the simple fact, that it took the Son of God's life to make it possible. To you, would you rather cast out demons, or make it to Heaven? I rest my case.

Day 30. Romans 8:18
"For I reckon that the sufferings of this present time are not worthy to be compared with the glory which shall be revealed in us."

Thought of the day: In life, we often find ourselves being attacked by the enemy. It can leave you drained and tired. By the Grace of God, America hasn't, as of yet, suffered like many other nations around the world for the Gospel. But no matter how hard the suffering might become; there is nothing greater than what awaits us when we are with Christ in Heaven. Keep your eyes focused on your new home when the enemy attacks, know that this is but for a season and then you will be home.

Overcoming Words for December

Chapter 13

Day 1. Psalm 25:4-5
"Shew me thy ways, O Lord; teach me thy paths. Lead me in thy truth, and teach me: for thou art the God of my salvation; on thee do I wait all the day."

Thought of the day: The Holy Spirit has been sent to guide us into all truths. No matter if it's what job to have or who to marry; He is there to lead us in the right paths in life. The problem is, most of us don't take the time to ask for that guidance. It's always best to wait on Him before making our decisions.

Day 2. Luke 12:25-26
"And which of you with taking thought can add to his stature one cubit? If ye then be not able to do that thing which is least, why take ye thought for the rest?"

Thought of the day: When we think of it, there is not much in this life that we truly have control of. I myself, would rather be tall, dark and handsome, or at least have my hair back! That is why it is so important to trust in the one who can override the boundaries we have in life. One who already knows what is ahead. Stop trusting in yourself and trust in God.

Day 3. Luke 10:41-42

"And Jesus answered and said unto her, Martha, Martha, thou art careful and troubled about many things: But one thing is needful: and Mary hath chosen that good part, which shall not be taken away from her."

Thought of the day: Because of our society and the cost to keep up; it has left us with little time left at the end of the day. We work, come home, eat, and go to bed. Then finally, when we get toward the end of our life, we realize that we wasted so many times we should have been with our family or working for Christ. Anything that we will have in Heaven will be things we have done for Christ on earth. Don't let time pass you by and be penniless for eternity in Heaven as far as the rewards for what you did for Christ while here on earth.

Day 4. Genesis 50:20

"But as for you, ye thought evil against me; but God meant it unto good, to bring to pass, as it is this day, to save much people alive."

Thought of the day: I can recall many times in my life, that Satan tried to destroy me. A lot of those times I may have brought on myself. But I thank God, that He has always turned those times around for my good when I would repent and walk in His Will. Nothing can happen to us, unless God allows it.

Day 5. 2 Corinthians 4:4
"In whom the god of this world hath blinded the minds of them which believe not, lest the light of the glorious gospel of Christ, who is the image of God, should shine unto them."

Thought of the day: Ever wondered why people can't see their need for Christ? It is because of their spiritual blindness. Satan gives them the promise of success and pleasure but doesn't let them see the end results. He makes them think they have life by the tail. It takes the Holy Spirit to open their eyes. You also have a part. The Bible says that we are the light of the world. If we are letting our light shine, then some may see the way. How bright is your light shining?

Day 6. Psalm 37:4
"Delight thyself also in the Lord: and he shall give thee the desires of thine heart."

Thought of the day: When we are sold out for God and love Him with all we have; we have peace and joy beyond comprehension. We would never want to do or ask anything that would displease Him. That is why God is able to give us the desires of our hearts because our hearts will be in tune with Him. Are your desires, something that God would desire for you?

Day 7. Ephesians 5:8
"For ye were sometimes darkness, but now are ye light in the Lord: walk as children of light:"

Thought of the day: Christ is the light, and in Him there is no darkness. Once He comes into our lives, we can then see just what a dark road we were traveling on. Thank God, He is the light unto our feet in this dark world we live in.

Day 8. 2 Peter 1:5
"And beside this, giving all diligence, add to your faith virtue; and to virtue knowledge;"

Thought of the day: God wants us to live our lives clean (virtuous) before Him and the world. To do this, we need to add knowledge (discernment), so we can see and know the dangers before we step into it.

Day 9. Matthew 10:29
"Are not two sparrows sold for a farthing? and one of them shall not fall on the ground without your Father."

Thought of the day: God loves all of His creation, but unlike the United States, which cares more for animals than human life, He cares for us so much more. You might feel He doesn't, but trust me, He has His all watchful eye on you!

Day 10. Psalm 100:4
"Enter into his gates with thanksgiving, and into his courts with praise: be thankful unto him, and bless his name."

Thought of the day: Even when Jesus taught us to pray, He showed us to start with giving God praise and thanks. We don't deserve anything in life. All that we have is a gift from God. Take the time to praise Him for all you have and thank Him for His all-sufficient power in your life. He deserves ALL the honor and praise.

Day 11. Romans 5:3
"And not only so, but we glory in tribulations also: knowing that tribulation worketh patience;"

Thought of the day: "Ouch!" How can we glory in tribulations? The tribulations here are the troubles and persecutions we receive because we are saved. The world hates us and will hate us even more as time goes on. If we can keep in mind, that this is for a moment, compared to eternity; we can rejoice to know we have an eternity free of suffering. The more God delivers us out of the enemies' hand, the more we trust God, and the more we can have the patience not only to bear our burden but care for the ones who are causing it. I'm glad this world is not my home.

Day 12. Hebrews 12:1
"Wherefore seeing we also are compassed about with so great a cloud of witnesses, let us lay aside every weight, and the sin which doth so easily beset us, and let us run with patience the race that is set before us,"

Thought of the day: I believe that the angels in Heaven are watching with anticipation on how well we run this race for God in life. We have only what they can dream of, Salvation. But I also believe that every one of our loved ones who have passed is watching with anticipation as well. They are now experiencing what one day we will experience. They know that Heaven is worth all we go through. I believe they are cheering us on. All eyes are on you! Run with all you have to win the race!

Day 13. Psalm 139:23
"Search me, O God, and know my heart: try me, and know my thoughts."

Thought of the day: Have you asked God to reveal to you your sins? More importantly, the hidden sins that you don't even know about. We need to keep our lives as pure as we can for God's Glory. Coming to God is more than just asking for things for ourselves, but also asking what He wants from us and to ask for cleansing so we can live our lives before others as we should.

Day 14. James 3:4-5
"Behold also the ships, which though they be so great, and are driven of fierce winds, yet are they turned about with a very small helm, whithersoever the governor listeth. Even so the tongue is a little member, and boasteth great things. Behold, how great a matter a little fire kindleth!"

Thought of the day: The tongue has caused war, pain, hurt, distrust, deception, but has also brought healing, encouragement, guidance. Everything in your life can change just by a single word from someone's tongue. You can also change a person's life with the words you say with your tongue. It is very powerful. Be careful how you use it.

Day 15. Ephesians 2:1
"And you hath he quickened, who were dead in trespasses and sins;"

Thought of the day: Like Lazarus in the tomb, we were dead spiritually. We couldn't see what sin was doing to us. But when you answer to Christ calling to come forth from the grave, you become alive! The joy of living flows through your veins. He not only gives us life but life more abundantly.

Day 16. Psalm 27:14
"Wait on the Lord: be of good courage, and he shall strengthen thine heart: wait, I say, on the Lord."

Thought of the day: The hardest thing for most of us is waiting. I can't count the times I jumped into a deal that they said had to be taken today, only to find myself bound to something for a long period of time and all the while it was costing me something. We need to wait on God's direction before we do anything. He will lead us into the right choices that will eventually bring a blessing, not a curse. It is so important that we wait, that here in this scripture it repeats itself. Wait, I say WAIT!

Day 17. Mark 8:29
"And he saith unto them, But whom say ye that I am? And Peter answereth and saith unto him, Thou art the Christ."

Thought of the day: The world has many ideas of who Jesus is. Some say He was a great teacher. Others believe He was just a normal person. Still, others, don't even believe He ever existed. Christ, when dealing with us, doesn't care what others think of Him; He wants to know who we believe He is. Do we really believe that He is the Son of God and can do what He claims He can do? Does your life reflect that you believe He is in control?

Day 18. James 4:14
"Whereas ye know not what shall be on the morrow. For what is your life? It is even a vapour, that appeareth for a little time, and then vanisheth away."

Thought of the day: Life is short. Handle it with prayer. Don't let life slip by living just for yourself. Live for others and God, and your life, in the end, will be full.

Day 19. Job 38:8-11
"Or who shut up the sea with doors, when it brake forth, as if it had issued out of the womb? When I made the cloud the garment thereof, and thick darkness a swaddlingband for it, And brake up for it my decreed place, and set bars and doors, And said, Hitherto shalt thou come, but no further: and here shall thy proud waves be stayed?"

Thought of the day: Being an ocean lover, I always look in amazement of how powerful that water is coming to shore, only for it to stop and go back. I have seen what the destruction can be when it overflows its banks. There is no greater power in all the earth than water. And yet, it must obey the voice of God. Morning after morning, you can tell exactly where it will stop until on those rare occasions, God allows it to overflow. If He can control the ocean waves, surely, he can control the storms in our lives when they come.

Day 20. Hebrews 4:16
"Let us therefore come boldly unto the throne of grace, that we may obtain mercy, and find grace to help in time of need."

Thought of the day: During the Old Testament times, some of the nation's kings wouldn't allow anyone to come to them unless he gave them permission. To do so without permission would mean instant death. But thanks to God through Jesus Christ, we can come to God's throne at any time and bring anything we might need to His attention. Let's never forget what a blessing that is. To have access to the throne 24/7.

Day 21. Hebrews 13:8
"Jesus Christ the same yesterday, and to day, and for ever."

Thought of the day: Our spouses change. Our friends change. Our jobs and health may change. And our financial situations may change; but isn't it good to know, that the one whom we need to trust the most, NEVER CHANGES. He is a steady rock that we can depend on forever.

Day 22. John 12:24

"Verily, verily, I say unto you, Except a corn of wheat fall into the ground and die, it abideth alone: but if it die, it bringeth forth much fruit."

Thought of the day: Sometimes in life, we must go through very hard times when we feel alone. It is a cold and dark time. It seems we have no hope or life within us. But it is during that time, that God is working in our lives for us to bring much fruit after we come through that valley. For us to do much for the Kingdom of God, we must die to ourselves, so that we can fruitful for God.

Day 23. Hebrews 12:11

"Now no chastening for the present seemeth to be joyous, but grievous: nevertheless afterward it yieldeth the peaceable fruit of righteousness unto them which are exercised thereby."

Thought of the day: I can't ever remember a time that I was about to get a spanking from my dad, that I said, "OH WOW! I have been waiting for this all day!" No, on the contrary, I was dreading it. But know that I am older, I understand that it was for my good and I can say now, that I am so glad that they took the time to discipline me in the past, so I can be a better person today.

Day 24. Matthew 23:37

"O Jerusalem, Jerusalem, thou that killest the prophets, and stonest them which are sent unto thee, how often would I have gathered thy children together, even as a hen gathereth her chickens under her wings, and ye would not!"

Thought of the day: Christ's heart breaks for us when we won't come to Him. He knows what Satan is trying to do and what your end will be if you don't repent and turn from the enemy. No matter how mean you are or what you have done, Christ is waiting to bring healing in your life.

Day 25. Romans 8:16
"The Spirit itself beareth witness with our spirit, that we are the children of God:"

Thought of the day: If you are truly a child of God, your life will show signs of it. It will be producing the Fruits of the Spirit, which are; love, joy, peace, long-suffering, gentleness, goodness, faith, meekness, and temperance. That doesn't mean you will always do it right, but your desire will be to do it. The Spirit will also bear witness by convicting us when we are about to sin. Is the Spirit bearing witness with yours that you have been born again?

Day 26. Hebrews 12:6
"For whom the Lord loveth he chasteneth, and scourgeth every son whom he receiveth."

Thought of the day: Sometimes God has to send us to the "woodshed." For those of you that don't know what that is, it is a term meaning to take a child to a place to get a spanking or be disciplined. I remember me thinking my parents must hate me when I got disciplined. But as an adult, I now know they were doing it so that I would learn a valuable lesson before I got myself into something I couldn't get out of. Don't get mad when God must take His belt to you. Be glad that He loves and cares for you enough to teach you how to live a life with less troubles.

Day 27. 1 Peter 2:9
"But ye are a chosen generation, a royal priesthood, an holy nation, a peculiar people; that ye should shew forth the praises of him who hath called you out of darkness into his marvellous light;"

Thought of the day: Once you become adopted into the Family of God, we change from an orphan to a member of the Royal Family. Now that we are a part of that family, we should try to act like royalty... Yes, people might treat us different, because now we act differently. We should be forever grateful that we are now a part of the Royal Family!

Day 28. James 1:17
"Every good gift and every perfect gift is from above, and cometh down from the Father of lights, with whom is no variableness, neither shadow of turning."

Thought of the day: Any gift given on earth will someday vanish or tarnish. Even when we give someone ourselves. But anything that God gives us will last forever. And of course, the best gift is the gift of Salvation. Do you have that gift yet?

Day 29. 2 Timothy 4:8
"Henceforth there is laid up for me a crown of righteousness, which the Lord, the righteous judge, shall give me at that day: and not to me only, but unto all them also that love his appearing."

Thought of the day: First, the crown mentioned is not like a crown a king would wear. It is a crown that especially runners would get in Rome for winning a race. Paul was about to die for his Faith, and he knew he had given his all in the race he ran. Therefore, he knew a crown was waiting for him. Can you say that you have a crown of righteousness laid up for you?

Day 30. 1 Corinthians 9:25
"And every man that striveth for the mastery is temperate in all things. Now they do it to obtain a corruptible crown, but we an incorruptible."

Thought of the day: In professional sports, each team gives it their all. They spend hours practicing and getting ready for the big game. Then when it is time to do their job, they fight to win. We, as Christians, have a much higher prize that we are striving for. Are you staying prepared to get out there and win, when your time is up to deliver your best?

Day 31. Jeremiah 6:16
"Thus saith the Lord, Stand ye in the ways, and see, and ask for the old paths, where is the good way, and walk therein, and ye shall find rest for your souls. But they said, We will not walk therein."

Thought of the day: Today, we find our nation doing things we never thought possible. Evil is running rampant. What is evil is called good, and what is good is called evil. God is calling us to repentance, and we are refusing to listen. We need to get back to the "Old Paths," the path of righteousness so God can once again bless us. You are about to enter a new year. Dedicate yourself in this new year to be a better Christian than you have ever been before. Commit yourself to do all that God asks you to do. Stay in prayer and in the Word of God so you can be found faithful and worthy and pray that God will send revival to heal our land.

Conclusion

I hope this book has given you encouragement this past year as you read from the pages of it. I also hope that it may have given you strength, hope, and comfort in times of need. But I would be remised if I didn't take out the time to ask you a very personal question. Do you know Jesus Christ as your personal Savior? Have you ever asked Him into your life and repented of your sin? If not, I want to give you some scriptures that can help you have a new life in Christ Jesus.

Did you know that you can know for sure that you are going to Heaven when you die? To do so, you must realize all of mankind are sinners. "For all have sinned and come short of the Glory of God" Romans 3:23. This would include you!

Did you know that there must be a price paid for sin and that payment is death? Romans 6:23 "For the wages of Sin is death; but the gift of God is eternal life through Jesus Christ our Lord" That is the price that all of mankind owed. Because of the Sin debt in your own personal life, you should pay the debt with your very life.

Did you know that there is a way where you don't have to give your life to pay the Sin debt that YOU owe? Romans 5:8 "But God commendeth his love toward us, in that while we were yet sinners, Christ died for us." Christ died for YOUR Sin debt, but there is something you must do, for that payment to be accepted.

You must agree with God that you are a sinner and in need of a Savior. You must be sorrowful for the condition you are in. You must agree that there is nothing in your power to be able to pay for the Sin debt that you owe. You must ask for Jesus to come into your life and to repent (turn away) from your sinful lifestyle. God will give you the power to do that.

It's not hard to do. It is as simple as this prayer. Will you say it with me? "Dear Lord Jesus. I know that I am a sinner. Please forgive me and come into my heart and save me right now. I know I am not worthy of this payment, but you have offered it, and right now, I am accepting that payment for me. Thank you, Lord, for saving my Soul and taking me in as your child. I will do my best to live for you this day forward."

If you said that prayer from your heart and truly meant it, you are now a born-again Christian. In Romans 10:13, the Bible says, "For whosoever shall call upon the name of the Lord, shall be saved." That is God's promise that He will save you if you call on Him. I want to be the first to welcome you into the family of God.

The next thing you need to do is find a good, Bible-believing church so that you can grow in your new Christian Faith. If you don't know where to go, contact us at www.treeoflifecoaching.org, and we will try our best to finding you a good church in your area.

I want to thank everyone who purchased this book. I hope it was a blessing to you, and please recommend it to others.

Made in the USA
Columbia, SC
13 September 2020